Matters of Degree

Also by Alan Jamieson

Hard Cash!

Which Subject? Which Career?*

Your Choice of A-Levels (with Mary Munro)

The *Which?* Guide to Sponsorship in Higher Education

*Published by Consumers' Association and Hodder & Stoughton in association with Hobsons Publishing PLC

Matters of Degree

Choosing and applying for a university or college course

Alan Jamieson

Student Helpbook Series

CRAC

© Hobsons Publishing PLC 1990, 1992, 1993

First published as *Your Choice of Degree and Diploma* 1982 by Hobsons Limited
Second edition 1985
Third edition 1987
Fourth edition published by Hobsons Publishing PLC 1990
Fifth edition published as *Matters of Degree* 1992
Sixth edition 1993

No part of this publication may be copied or reproduced, stored in a retrieval system or transmitted in any form or by any means electronic or mechanical or by photocopying, recording or otherwise without the prior permission of the publishers.

ISBN 1 85324 799 5

CRAC

The Careers Research and Advisory Centre (CRAC) is a registered educational charity. Hobsons Publishing PLC produces CRAC publications under exclusive licence and royalty agreements.

Printed and bound in Great Britain by Clays Ltd, St Ives plc, Bungay, Suffolk.

Ref. L136/ss 6 qq/J/JC

Acknowledgments

The author, editor and publishers are most grateful to the many individuals and organisations who have assisted in the preparation of this publication. These include admissions tutors of colleges and universities who replied to queries, and the following:

The Association of Commonwealth Universities
The Committee of Vice-Chancellors and Principals
The Universities and Colleges Admissions Service
The Universities Statistical Record
The Scottish Office Education Department
The Department for Education
The Standing Conference of Principals and Directors of Colleges and Institutes of Higher Education
The National Union of Students
The Central Bureau for Educational Visits & Exchanges
The Scottish Centrally Funded Colleges

With special thanks to:
Brendan Lehane, freelance journalist
David Elsom, educational consultant
Alison Foster, Tony Higgins and Phillip Oakley, UCAS

Contents

Introduction
Higher Education – Is It for Me?   9
The Flip Side   9

Part 1 Choosing
The World of Higher Education   15
Recent Changes in Higher Education   15
Your Place in Higher Education   16
Making Choices   17
The Extent of Your Choice   17
Where to Start   19
Who Am I?   22
Do I Have the Grades?   24
What Am I Going to Study?   28
Where Am I Going to Study?   34
Affiliated and Associate Colleges and Franchised Courses   48
An Eye to a Career   49
Where College Meets Work: Sandwich Courses   58
Looking for Sponsorship? A Way to Pay for College   61
Professional and Vocational Courses   63
A Year Abroad – Studying   63
Qualifications to Choose Between   65
How Long Does HE Take?   68
Course Comparisons: Six Important Points   69
A Word about Art and Design Courses   74
Teaching and Learning: Structures and Styles   75
Methods of Assessment   83
Non-academic Criteria   84
Disabled Students   89
Mature Students   90
Overseas Students   91
Conclusion   95

Part 2 UCAS – Application Procedures
Introduction   101
Making Your Application   101

Before Completing the UCAS Form	102
Filling in the UCAS Form	103
When to Apply	110
After You Apply – the UCAS Timetable	112
Conditional Offers	113
Confirmation of Offers	114
Clearing	114
Applying to Cambridge and Oxford	116
Courses Leading to the Basic Professional Social Work Qualification	117
England, Northern Ireland, Scotland and Wales	117
The Chance of Succeeding	119
Visits and Open Days	126
Interviews	127

Part 3 Accommodation, Money, the Gap Year

Typical Accommodation	132
Allocation of Places	134
Fees and Charges	136
Vacations	137
Problems in Finding Accommodation	137
Small Towns	137
Big City Life!	138
Paying Your Way	139
The Council Tax	143
A Year Off	143
Fit for Adventure	145

Part 4 Where to Find Out More

Address List	149
Book List	150
The Higher Education Institutions: Names, Addresses, Telephone Numbers	159

Glossary of Terms and Abbreviations   179

Introduction

Higher Education – Is It for Me?

There has never been a more exciting time to enter higher education. The variety of courses and changes in the system as a whole are greater than ever before. Those entering higher education in the 1990s are able to choose between new courses and flexible programmes of work; large campus universities or small, town-based colleges; vocational degrees in specific subjects or broad-based combined studies courses. As never before, the choice is yours.

Achieving a degree or diploma is valued for numerous reasons. There are still jobs from which you will be excluded if you don't have a degree, and usually a graduate is able to start a career at a higher level than a non-graduate. Far fewer people go on to study after their first degree than start work at that point, so having a degree puts you on a par with, or above, the majority of your age group.

If you aren't swayed by career prospects, then consider that at this stage of education, you may have more opportunities for non-academic activities than at any other time of your life. You could find yourself parachuting, debating, running the college magazine, campaigning for famine relief, raising funds for charity, lying in the sun by the pool, dancing all night, having a bed race round the town, playing an instrument in a sound-proofed studio, or even enjoying using the library! You will probably make discoveries about yourself that life in a job begun at 18 would not have made possible. Besides, a regular job should await you further down the line.

The Flip Side

A degree is not a guarantee of success. There is evidence of considerable dissatisfaction among graduates with the jobs they get, especially during their early working years. You may make your fortune without one – the 1990s can boast a prime minister who left school at sixteen, and numerous entrepreneurs have succeeded without letters after their names. Degrees proliferate among the big names in art, music, writing, television and film-making, but not enough to allow any firm correlation between qualifications and success.

There are some with reason to know who argue that the university's attention to the intellect suppresses and inhibits natural feelings and their expression, and that years of argument and nit-picking can destroy the creative spark.

Higher education postpones things that, to some anyway, are irresistibly attractive: money, home, the challenge of getting on, marrying, having a family, or possessing skills and abilities which college life is unlikely to foster – though the number of these is decreasing as the scope of higher education broadens.

These two 'HE in a nutshell' views are only included to point out that there are standard attitudes to higher education and that on balance if HE is an option you should take it. You are unlikely to have the chance later on to experience the lifestyle and opportunity for study it affords. Almost certainly, you will benefit both in your career and personally.

Just what students of 16, 17 and 18 know about HE varies enormously. Views range from 'I'm going to be an X, so I'm doing these A-levels and this degree at this college', to 'HE? Yes, but I'm not going!' Often, whether or not students go on to study at 18 is due to the attitudes they grow up surrounded with, from family, friends, the type of school they attend, and so on. Often it is not an accurate reflection of their ability to gain a diploma or degree.

In this book we present the notion that to have the chance of continuing your education is a cause for celebration. It's up to you to make sure that you make the right choices about how to spend the next three or four years of your life. You'll need a lot more information than the superficial knowledge of the nutshell, and this book provides it.

If you have your future mapped out, you can just take the facts: how to apply; the deadlines; the statistics on how far you can get on three Cs, and so on. You could also sneak a glance at Part I on 'Choosing' and make sure you're heading the right way for the right reasons. If, on the other hand, you draw a blank when you think about HE, you could sit down with this book, a pen and some paper, and find out what HE's got to offer you, what you might study, and where. This book isn't going to give you the name of a course and an institution – better than that, it can help you identify what you are looking for in terms of the kind of assessment you can best handle; the kind of HE institutions you should be considering; where you can go with the grades you expect to gain; how you are going to finance yourself; and more. It throws up all the considerations you have to take into account and gives you the information to make a decision about them. Where appropriate it points you in the direction of specialist sources of information: *Degree Course Guides* to help you compare the courses offered in each degree subject with one another; books describing sponsorship opportunities if that's what you need; and so on. After working through *Matters of Degree* you should be able to go to your careers teacher or adviser or a prospectus knowing the features you want in a course. With all the information systems available today, such as the ECCTIS UK Courses Database, that is enough of a lead for possible courses to jump out at you and fill your UCAS form.

With a get-up-and-go approach to finding out about HE and doing certain basic things right, like getting your application form in early and making the effort to see the places you have in mind, you will find a course that suits you.

Some readers will find that they like the sound of this, but now is not the right time. Other things beckon. A year off, a chance of a job, whatever. Maybe HE is something for later. It is becoming easier to be a mature student (aged 21 and over at the start of the course). Reduced course fees and assistance from college funds are available to help Access students (people who want to take an HE course but lack A-levels). Access funds are now available to help students with particular financial problems, and students with family commitments are often given priority. Repayments on Career Development Loans don't begin until three months after your course has finished, and Student Loans are available. Modular courses with self-contained units of study are more flexible than traditional courses and may suit people weaving a course around other commitments.

Whatever your view of HE, the aim of *Matters of Degree* is to add enough to your understanding to make your admission to HE a certainty.

Matters of Degree is in four parts:

Part 1 is all about choosing. It asks you to look at yourself so that the choices you make are realistic in terms of your skills, achievements and aspirations. It looks at all the choices on offer to you by running through the ranges of teaching styles, methods of assessment, degrees, diplomas, professional courses, sandwich courses and so on. All jargon is explained and there's a glossary at the back of the book. Part 1 is intended to prepare you for the next stage: applying for a place.

INTRODUCTION

Part 2 explains the procedures involved in making applications. At this stage you don't just want to get in *somewhere*; you want to get the place you hope for. Pitching the application at the right level – not too high in case of refusal, but not too low either because you can never be sure that luck, charm, personality or quick wits will not get you in where exam results alone would not – requires careful thought. This section also deals with visits and interviews.

The visits and/or interview are important. You are being assessed and have the chance to assess your interviewer and the institution he or she represents. As the answers to your questions might tip the scales for you, they are of paramount importance. Part 2 suggests the points you may need to find out at interview, how to remember them when there are all sorts of things to distract you, and how to project the best aspects of yourself.

Part 3 moves on to the period after acceptance: you're in – you're almost a student. Here we cover issues such as finding accommodation, preparing for life away from home, and for a new programme of work. We also focus on money matters: discussing the fees for your course, the cost of residence, of meals and food, books, stationery, travel, clothes, entertainment and so on. We take a hard look at sources of money: grants and awards from local education authorities, scholarships, Student Loans, the banks, ways of earning money, and how to economise.

An increasing number of school-leavers choose to take a year off before entering higher education. Part 3 discusses the pros and cons of this kind of break.

Part of the function of this book is to point you in the right direction at important junctures, and to recommend other books and organisations able to fill in the details of the general picture. In **Part 4** we list all these books and addresses, for easy reference. This section follows up all the books mentioned throughout the text and includes a glossary on page 179. The meaning of every technical word is explained here.

1. *Choosing*

The World of Higher Education

Within a generation, the number of people entering higher education has risen from one in twenty to one in five. Between 1980 and 1992 there was a 56 per cent increase in the numbers of students in full-time higher education. Suddenly, the world of higher education has been opened up to many more people and is rapidly expanding. Indeed, in the autumn of 1992 the Government grew anxious about the speed and cost of the growth. The Higher Education Funding Councils were told to cut back on plans for expansion. The new objective was to increase the number of students in further education by eight per cent a year for each of the next three years.

This change of policy means that it will be tougher to get a place in HE. Your grades will have to be better, that is, good A-level (or AS) scores with As and Bs rather than Cs.

Another big change came in 1992 with the change of name for the polytechnics. For 25 years there had been older universities and the younger polytechnics; in 1992 the polytechnics took new titles, so creating 96 UK universities and university colleges.

Recent Changes in Higher Education

You may have read in the newspapers about 'cuts' in the money provided by the Government for universities. They aren't really cuts. There isn't a bottomless pool of money for universities, so the Government rations yearly grants by a complex funding system. The universities — like the further education colleges which became independent institutions in April 1993 — have to manage with the money they are given. Unfortunately, funds are not as generous as they would wish.

Your Place in Higher Education

As the universities put a freeze on the number of places, the number of applicants continues to grow. This means that there is great competition for places.

Let's look at some facts. More than 374,000 applicants submitted multiple applications for places to universities and colleges. Within two years, the number of applicants is expected to rise to 420,000. That is, six per cent more students apply each year. But the number of places is growing only by between one and two per cent.

Many students will be disappointed. It is anticipated that 135,000 applicants each year do not obtain a place because their A-level or other exam grades are not high enough, or there simply aren't enough places.

Candidates face the most severe competition for arts, social science and teacher-training courses. The Government, through its funding system, favours students who apply for science, technology, and engineering courses. You will find it rather easier to get a place on one of these than on an arts course.

Now for the good news: the universities and colleges are continually adapting courses to match industrial and social needs. This means that attractive new degree and HND courses in vocational subjects, in media studies, and in new technology topics such as biotechnology are being devised. Furthermore, universities are increasingly making arrangements with local further and higher education colleges to 'franchise' their courses. This means that more institutions can offer all or part of a degree course. (See page 48, 'Affiliated and Associate Colleges and Franchised Courses'.)

Making Choices

Before we deal with the process of choosing, let us establish what we mean by 'choosing'? In this instance it means deciding on a course, changing your mind, or being turned down, then choosing again. Many factors beyond your control, as well as your own changes of heart, may lead you to a new track at some stage. It is just as well to be prepared for change, and in many cases it may lead you to a new opportunity. Being inflexibly resolved cuts down the scope for a happy chance find; a subject or a college that you have never seriously thought of before and which was far from being your first choice, may in the event turn out to be ideally suited to you. There are, after all, plenty of thriving subjects – metallurgy, polymer science, media studies, and many languages – that are usually not offered at school and which invariably represent some sort of gamble on the student's part. Choosing, in short, is a tricky business.

The Extent of Your Choice

Some of the choosing, of course, is done for you by the selection processes of the colleges themselves. The criteria they work on are in the main academic. To these may be added the impression you make at an interview, and your interests and achievements (as in sport, say, or extra-curricular activities such as journalism and acting). But high grades in examinations usually come first.

That still leaves you with the key questions:
1. **Do I have the *grades*?**
2. ***What* am I going to study?**
3. ***Where* am I going to study?**
4. **How will it help my *career*? Or will it lead to a career?**
5. **What *qualification* am I going to leave with?**

The decisions she was being forced to make suddenly seemed overwhelming.

6. How *long* is it going to take?
7. Do I have the *right* qualifications to apply?
8. How am I going to *pay* for the course?

As you work your way through *Matters of Degree*, you will have the opportunity to tackle these questions. Use the chart on pages 20 and 21 to help you focus on issues. When you reach the end of Part 1, you should have a much better idea of how to complete it. When choosing your higher education course and college, you naturally want everything to match your tastes: course, location, teachers, view from your window, and all the rest. This is not usually possible; it is simply asking too much. But if you worry less about minor criteria you will be more likely to find a course that answers the major ones to your satisfaction.

Where to Start

One starting point is the subject or subjects you will study. With that resolved, other questions should fall into place. Your subject choice will point you in the direction of the institutions where you can study the particular areas of your subjects which you favour, eg a period in history, or particular authors or an attractive match of several different subjects. You may find courses in a number of places that you like, and at that stage you need to be able to compare them. The CRAC *Degree Course Guides* will help here. They give course comparisons in single subjects and really illuminate just how different your experience could be studying engineering at Bristol as opposed to, say, Exeter. Or indeed it may be that the attraction of extra-curricular opportunities helps you rank your choice of institutions. What's on offer in this area will be in the colleges' free prospectuses. At the back of this book you'll find addresses to write to for the prospectuses.

Many students, however, just cannot be that specific. For them a broad look at the criteria for choosing may cause some factors to stand out as priorities. That's why Part I runs through the whole range of HE options.

However you intend to tackle the choosing process, the first stage is to assemble useful data. This book is your starting point and will tell you where you need to look at subsequent stages. The first thing to do is to talk about higher education. Take advice and information from teachers, parents, family and friends and, if possible, students who are or have recently been at establishments which interest you. Build yourself a picture of what higher education is all about. You may be able to get to one of the exhibitions held in some of the bigger cities each spring. At around the same time most higher education institutions have open days at which lecturers and students are

Where-to-study chart

Here is a summary of some of the factors to consider before choosing a place to study. To help you towards a decision place ticks to reflect your preferences.

1 Course

	2-year	3-year	4-year	Sandwich	Other
BA in single subject	☐	☐	☐	☐	☐
BSc	☐	☐	☐	☐	☐
BEd	☐	☐	☐	☐	☐
BA/BSc in joint-study courses	☐	☐	☐	☐	☐
BA/BSc in combined studies	☐	☐	☐	☐	☐
DipHE	☐	☐	☐	☐	☐
BTEC higher national diploma	☐	☐	☐	☐	☐

2 Institution
- University ☐
- College/Institute of HE ☐
- FE college ☐
- Art college ☐

3 Location
- City precinct ☐
- Suburban ☐
- Town centre ☐
- Rural ☐
- Campus ☐
- Near own home ☐

4 Geography
- Scotland ☐
- Wales ☐
- Northern Ireland ☐
- London ☐
- South of England ☐
- Midlands ☐
- North of England ☐

5 Size
- Over 10,000 students ☐
- 5,000 to 10,000 students ☐
- 2,000 to 5,000 students ☐
- Less than 2,000 students ☐

6 Accommodation
- In-college residence ☐
- Halls of residence ☐
- Lodgings ☐
- Flats ☐
- At home ☐

PART 1·CHOOSING

7 Student life
Sports facilities ☐
Student health service ☐
Social and cultural facilities ☐
Mixed sexes (equal proportion of men and women) ☐

8 Study facilities
Can transfer to different course ☐
Library/lab/workshop/studio ☐
Formal teaching methods ☐
Informal teaching methods ☐

During those afternoons spent taking tea with Mrs B, Gerald felt the first stirring of a new social awareness.

available to answer questions. It pays here to be armed with questions, and to bear in mind that staff and students will on balance promote their own institution. Your school or college should have written information and videos in the careers office, and you should make use of your local careers service.

When you are familiar with the range of courses in higher education, turn to books to investigate the queries thrown up by discussion. The 'Book List' in Part 4 includes all books we recommend throughout *Matters of Degree*, and many are accompanied by a brief description.

This book will help you build your higher education picture, a picture of yourself and point you in the direction of further information and advice.

Who Am I?

Since there are so many courses available to you, it is hardly possible to study them all and choose between them. Far better to study yourself and match your qualifications and ambitions to what's on offer. That will give you a shorter list of possibilities to consider seriously. Remember though, that you are not involved in a hunt for a single elusive course. Any one of a number of courses will probably suit you.

You need to create an accurate self-portrait – a frank assessment of your abilities, qualifications, interests, hopes and ambitions. Fill in the chart opposite. It will make you clearer about relevant aspects of yourself. It will be useful, when you come to short-list your options, to check that everything you have put down here is taken into account. It may even remind you of qualities, preferences and quirks you might otherwise have overlooked. It can be modified or added to at any stage.

Defining yourself is difficult and open-ended; the 'you' on paper today will be different a year from now, and you should leave room for the unexpected, the inspired, or the chance of conversion to a different path. Sometimes, too, it is best not to 'go with the flow' but to keep an open mind, to examine all possibilities, however bright, exotic or incongruous.

Why study for a degree or diploma?

Mark each box with a tick or cross to show if you agree with the statements.

- [ ] I enjoy studying
- [ ] I'm keen to add to my knowledge
- [ ] I'm expecting to gain personal satisfaction from studying
- [ ] My teachers think I have the ability to gain a degree
- [ ] My parents want me to take a degree or diploma course
- [ ] My friends think I should go on to college
- [ ] I want to continue with a subject I really enjoy
- [ ] I think that to get a good job you must be highly qualified
- [ ] I want to teach this subject
- [ ] I want to take up a completely new subject or course
- [ ] I want to take a mixed course of several subjects
- [ ] I feel I must get away from home
- [ ] I want to challenge myself, develop new skills
- [ ] I have a particular career in view and need a degree or diploma to get started
- [ ] I want to put off making a career decision
- [ ] I don't want to start a job just yet
- [ ] I want to enjoy the social life of college
- [ ] I'm looking forward to the cultural life of college
- [ ] I'm keen on sport
- [ ] I want to find new friends
- [ ] I don't know what to do, but I'm capable of studying further
- [ ] I think it's an opportunity, and I may never have the chance again

Look at your completed chart and see how many of these common reasons for going into higher education apply to you. Judge whether you have enough positive academic reasons, as well as the social and cultural. Judge too whether higher education is something you want for yourself, or something the people who influence you – your parents, teachers, friends, etc – are pushing you towards. Although their opinions are worth hearing, as you work through the application process you should feel that you are in control of the decisions made about the next few years of your life.

Do I Have the Grades?
A-level qualifications

Every institution requires evidence of a good general all-round education. This is usually called the 'general requirement'. It normally means passes in two A-levels and three other subjects at GCSE. This will make you eligible for:

- **Degree courses at universities and colleges.**
- **Diploma of higher education courses, available at most colleges and institutes of higher education.**
- **Advanced courses at universities and colleges, leading to college diplomas and certificates.**
- **Teacher-training. For this, as well as A-level passes you will need good GCSE passes in three other subjects including English language and mathematics.**
- **Foundation courses in art and design that can lead directly to degree or HND courses in design.**

Some courses specify the subjects in which they require GCSE and A-level passes. More on this later. You should note that two A-levels is the minimum requirement and higher

PART 1 • CHOOSING

A frisson swept through the little group as, with trembling hands, Charlotte opened the envelope.

grades will get you further: three specific A-level passes (four Highers) is generally the standard against which you will be competing.

Other recognised qualifications
>ASs
>Scottish Higher Grade and the Certificate of Sixth Year Studies
>BTEC (SCOTVEC) national certificate or national diploma
>BTEC higher national diploma
>BTEC higher national certificate
>The International General Certificate of Secondary Education is recognised as equivalent to GCSE.
>(Two AS passes count as the equivalent of one A-level.)

There are exemptions for adults who have no formal qualifications but have taken 'Access' or other preliminary courses. There is a *Courses Directory* of Access courses, published by ECCTIS.

One A-level

If you have one A-level pass, plus three GCSEs at grades A, B or C, these courses are open to you at universities and colleges:

- **BTEC and SCOTVEC higher national diploma courses in a wide range of subjects. For these courses you are normally expected to have studied two A-level subjects and passed at least one of them.**

GCSEs

If you have no passes at A-level, but have at least four GCSE passes at grades A to C (including English and maths) you can enter courses leading to the City and Guilds of London Institute awards, BTEC national certificates and national diplomas and GNVQ courses that will ultimately replace national diplomas. You can study national diploma courses in art and design, engineering, sciences and other subjects. Such courses are available at colleges of art, colleges of building, printing, design and technology, and some universities.

CATS

CATS means Credit Accumulation and Transfer. The idea behind it is that prior experience, company training and qualifications taken some time ago should all count in favour of a course applicant. This experience and training are the 'credits'. 'Accumulation' means that the experience is put on a record of achievement and 'transfer' takes place when the person moves from his or her job and applies for a course. You can find out about CATS by consulting *The Students' Guide to Educational Credit Transfer*, from ECCTIS.

PART 1 • CHOOSING

Which subjects are essential?
Degree courses in arts subjects

The course requirements are usually a pass at A-level in the same subject as the intended degree ('usually', because there are always special cases). For a foreign language, if a student has shown outstanding ability at A-level in traditional language courses, such as French or German, the student may be allowed to start a new language from scratch. For the following degree courses, however, it is generally required that an applicant has an A-level in the same subject.

English	Greek	Latin
French	History	
Geography	Italian	
German	Spanish	

Degree courses in science subjects

The course requirement is usually an A-level pass in the subject concerned or a closely related subject. If there is a clear match between A-level and degree course, an A-level pass is generally required (biology, maths, etc). For degree courses listed below, three good A-level passes are normally required and sometimes two passes are asked for in named subjects, usually maths (in any form – pure, applied, etc), physics, chemistry and biology. There are, however, some engineering courses specifically designed for students without maths and/or science at A-level.

Agriculture	Environmental sciences
Astronomy	Ergonomics
Biochemistry	Geology
Biophysics	Human sciences
Botany	Marine biology
Computer science	Mathematics
Dentistry	Medicine

Engineering
- acoustic
- aeronautical
- automotive
- chemical
- civil
- computer
- electrical
- electronic
- manufacturing
- marine
- mechanical
- production, etc

Metallurgy
Natural sciences
Optics
Pharmacy
Psychology (BSc)
Statistics
Surveying
- building
- quantity
Textile technology
Zoology

There are only two choices of paramount importance: what to study, and where. Let's deal with the first.

What Am I Going to Study?

Your choice of subject or a group of subjects may be closely linked with your reasons for going on to higher education. You may want to pursue a particular subject because you want to know more about it and you like the kind of studying it involves, such as a lot of reading or practical experiments or physical activity. Or maybe the subject will develop your social skills through contact with people on work placements, through giving seminars, or taking a dramatic production 'on the road'. A subject can offer you a lot besides its facts and knowledge. A good course will enable you to develop strengths you can already identify as well as present new challenges to broaden your achievements.

If you have an idea of your skills and the qualities you have, you may be looking for a course that will build on those skills. Thinking of a particular career may be a secondary issue to your personal development.

On the other hand, a higher education qualification may be a springboard into a career. For example, a law degree gains you exemption from the one-year conversion course which other undergraduates must take. A law graduate may go straight into a single year of training to become a barrister or solicitor. Similarly, a four-year teaching degree (a Bachelor of Education) will enable you to begin teaching upon graduating, whereas other undergraduates generally take a one-year postgraduate teaching certificate before they start teaching in the state system.

Look at this checklist and consider whether it stimulates your enthusiasm for any subjects or, more importantly, skills you wish to improve or acquire.

- [ ] **I need this subject for my career**
- [ ] **I was good at this subject at school**
- [ ] **I'd like to understand the world of work**
- [ ] **I'm fascinated by figures**
- [ ] **I'm artistic**
- [ ] **I want to create**
- [ ] **I want a career in outdoor activities, or sports**
- [ ] **I'm good at explaining things to people**
- [ ] **I can be very persuasive**
- [ ] **I want to work with people**
- [ ] **I want to work with books, print, words**
- [ ] **I'd like to mix academic study with some experience of work**

This kind of list is endless. As you mark this one, think of other statements you could apply to yourself. You are assessing your strengths and linking them to the skills required in your life after college. If you have some careers in mind, or can think of skills you'd like to use in your working life, work backwards to the course which will get you to that position.

Alternatively, start with where you are now and aim to develop some strengths which you'd like to possess.

Add other statements to the list to which you can answer yes or no. Discuss your list with someone who knows you well. Then extract from it a list of skills, or areas of knowledge or ability which you can see yourself pursuing. If you think this selection represents your interests, discuss it with a careers adviser to find out how it relates to various jobs and careers.

If you are interested in taking a combination of arts and science subjects at A-level, here are some courses open to you.

Accountancy	Fine Art
American studies	Land economy
Archaeology	Linguistics
Architecture	Management
Building studies	Politics
Catering studies	Public administration
Computer studies	Sociology
Divinity	Theatre studies
Education	Town and country-planning

The range of subjects is vast: over 11,500 first-degree courses are on offer at universities, and colleges offer a similar range. You don't know what you could miss if you don't do some research!

The following is a more detailed breakdown of subjects within broad areas of study. Go through the list. In each of the boxes, write **1**, **2**, or **3**:

1 = I am very interested in this subject or course
2 = I am interested in this subject or course and would like to know more about it
3 = I am not interested or qualified to take this subject or course

- ☐ A broad general degree course covering several subjects
- ☐ A combined sciences course covering several subjects
- ☐ A combined arts course covering several subjects

Architecture and land
- ☐ Architecture
- ☐ Land economy and estate management
- ☐ Planning: town and country
- ☐ Surveying: general building and quantity

Arts and humanities
- ☐ A general arts or humanities course
- ☐ American studies
- ☐ Archaeology
- ☐ English literature
- ☐ History (ancient, medieval, modern – write in your preference)
- ☐ Philosophy
- ☐ Religious studies/theology

Business and management studies
- ☐ Accountancy and finance
- ☐ Administration
- ☐ Business studies
- ☐ Hotel and catering administration and management
- ☐ Management
- ☐ Public administration

with options in:
- ☐ Advertising
- ☐ Marketing
- ☐ Public relations
- ☐ Retailing

Classical languages, classical civilisation and ancient British languages
- ☐ Anglo-Saxon
- ☐ Celtic/Welsh/Irish
- ☐ Classical civilisation
- ☐ Classics
- ☐ Latin and/or Greek
- ☐ Scottish studies

A communication studies course
- ☐ Communication and media studies
- ☐ Drama
- ☐ Film and television
- ☐ Music
- ☐ Photography
- ☐ Publishing
- ☐ Visual communications technology

A creative arts course
- [ ] Art and design
- [ ] Art history
- [ ] Ceramics and glass design
- [ ] Fine art
- [ ] Furniture design
- [ ] Graphic design
- [ ] Interior design
- [ ] Silver and jewellery
- [ ] Textile and fashion design

Engineering
- [ ] Aeronautical
- [ ] Automotive
- [ ] Chemical
- [ ] Civil and structural
- [ ] Computer and control systems
- [ ] Electrical
- [ ] Engineering design
- [ ] Environmental (public health)
- [ ] Marine
- [ ] Mechanical
- [ ] Mining and minerals
- [ ] Naval architecture and shipbuilding
- [ ] Production

Geography and earth sciences
- [ ] Earth sciences
- [ ] Environmental sciences
- [ ] Environmental studies
- [ ] Geography
- [ ] Geology

Industrial technologies
- [ ] Building: services and engineering
- [ ] Economics
- [ ] Fuel and energy
- [ ] Glass
- [ ] Marine
- [ ] Materials
- [ ] Metallurgy
- [ ] Paper
- [ ] Printing
- [ ] Textile and clothing
- [ ] Transport

Languages
- [ ] African studies
- [ ] East European languages (write in which one(s), eg Russian, Polish, Czech)
- [ ] English language
- [ ] Latin American studies
- [ ] Linguistics
- [ ] Modern West European languages (write in which one(s), eg Dutch, French, Spanish)
- [ ] Oriental studies

- ☐ Other languages (choose which one(s), eg Arabic, Hebrew, Japanese)
- ☐ Scandinavian languages (choose which one(s), eg Norwegian, Swedish, Danish)

Librarianship
- ☐ Information science or technology
- ☐ Librarianship

Medicine and medicinal sciences
- ☐ Anatomy
- ☐ Dentistry
- ☐ Medical studies
- ☐ Medicine
- ☐ Nursing studies
- ☐ Occupational therapy
- ☐ Ophthalmic optics (optometry)
- ☐ Pharmacology
- ☐ Pharmacy
- ☐ Physiotherapy
- ☐ Speech therapy/speech sciences

Sciences – biological
- ☐ Biochemistry
- ☐ Biology
- ☐ Biophysics
- ☐ Botany
- ☐ Dietetics
- ☐ Food science and nutrition
- ☐ Genetics
- ☐ Home economics
- ☐ Marine biology
- ☐ Microbiology
- ☐ Physiology
- ☐ Zoology

Sciences – human
- ☐ Behavioural sciences
- ☐ Psychology

Sciences – mathematical
- ☐ Computer science
- ☐ Mathematics
- ☐ Statistics

Sciences – physical and chemical
- ☐ Acoustics
- ☐ Astrophysics
- ☐ Chemical physics
- ☐ Chemistry
- ☐ Electronics
- ☐ Meteorology
- ☐ Oceanography
- ☐ Physics

Social sciences, government and law
- ☐ Anthropology
- ☐ Community studies

- ☐ Economic and social history
- ☐ Economics
- ☐ International relations
- ☐ Law
- ☐ Peace studies
- ☐ Politics and government
- ☐ Social administration
- ☐ Social work
- ☐ Sociology
- ☐ Youth studies/youth work

Sports and recreation
- ☐ Dance and movement
- ☐ Physical education
- ☐ Science and sport and recreation
- ☐ Sports management

A course leading to teaching
- ☐ A BEd degree
- ☐ A DipHE course, leading to a BEd
- ☐ A subject course, followed by a one-year postgraduate course for a certificate in education (PGCE)
- ☐ What subject(s) would you like to teach?

Where Am I Going to Study?

You can study for a first degree or diploma at a university, at a college or institute of higher education, or at a college of further education. You may find that your choice of course points you in the direction of certain institutions. Some places have gained good reputations for particular courses, and, more generally, the different types of institution have strengths you should be aware of.

Take, for example, vocational qualifications. These are currently in vogue. And for good reason. With the numbers of graduates rising, and fighting each other for jobs, those with the head start are the students whose courses are related to commerce and industry. They know how the world of work functions and will be in a position to make a financial contribution to the companies they join more quickly than

PART 1 · CHOOSING

'Will you have to speak French there, Louise?' 'Oh no, Jimmy! De Montfort's a university in Leicester', explained his sister.

someone with a purely academic qualification. The specialist providers of this kind of higher education are generally the newer universities and the former polytechnics.

Universities

There are 96 universities and university colleges. They are concerned with scholarship, that is, the study in depth of a subject or a topic within a subject. Universities are also research institutions where staff are concerned with extending knowledge, developing new ideas and examining existing ones. Lastly, they are heavily involved in teaching, which is the area you, as an undergraduate, will be most interested in. It used to be the case that university lecturers were often remote from industry and commerce. Today, however, many departments and staff have close connections with industry, and many courses lead directly into particular jobs in industry.

The location of the older universities

Key

England
1 Aston University
2 University of Bath
3 University of Birmingham
4 University of Bradford
5 University of Bristol
6 Brunel University
7 University of Buckingham
8 University of Cambridge
9 City University
10 Cranfield Institute of Technology
11 University of Durham
12 University of East Anglia
13 University of Essex
14 University of Exeter
15 University of Hull
16 Keele University
17 University of Kent at Canterbury
18 University of Lancaster
19 University of Leeds
20 University of Leicester
21 University of Liverpool
22 University of London
23 Loughborough University of Technology
24 University of Manchester
25 University of Manchester Institute of Science and Technology
26 University of Newcastle upon Tyne
27 University of Nottingham
28 Open University
29 University of Oxford
30 University of Reading
31 University of Salford
32 University of Sheffield
33 University of Southampton
34 University of Surrey
35 University of Sussex
36 University of Warwick
37 University of York

Scotland
38 University of Aberdeen
39 University of Dundee
40 University of Edinburgh
41 University of Glasgow
42 Heriot-Watt University
43 University of St Andrews
44 University of Stirling
45 University of Strathclyde

Wales
46 University College of Wales, Aberystwyth

47 University of Wales, Bangor
48 University of Wales College of Cardiff
49 University of Wales College of Medicine
50 St David's University College, Lampeter
51 University College of Swansea

Northern Ireland
52 Queen's University of Belfast
53 University of Ulster, Coleraine

Universities create their own courses and award their own degrees. Each university is independent and, to a large extent, makes its own rules. They are unique institutions and for students who are fortunate enough to study there, they provide a privileged start in life.

London University colleges

The London University colleges vary in size and in the courses they offer. There are colleges, schools, institutes and teaching hospitals.

Courtauld Institute of Art
Goldsmiths' College
Heythorp College
Imperial College of Science, Technology and Medicine
Jews' College
King's College
London School of Economics and Political Science
Queen Mary and Westfield College
Royal Holloway and Bedford New College
Royal Veterinary College
School of Oriental and African Studies
School of Pharmacy
School of Slavonic and East European Studies
University College
Wye College
Medical and dental schools
Birkbeck College (part-time only)

The 'new' universities – formerly polytechnics

As a consequence of the 1992 Further and Higher Education Act, the former polytechnics were designated as universities. Some of the larger colleges of higher education were also awarded university status. The former polytechnics have chosen new names (see pages 42 and 43).

These new universities are also concerned with scholarship, research and teaching. In the past most polytechnic courses were heavily vocational; the polytechnics were strong in subjects like business studies, management, and engineering. Today, these new universities also offer courses similar to those provided in the 'old' universities: history, geography, English, languages, social sciences. They include schools of art, and provide educational courses leading to the BEd (teaching degree) and other qualifications. The wide range of their courses and their vocational strengths explain the success of the former polytechnics. They offer degrees, diplomas, certificates and all kinds of professional and vocational training courses. At older universities, where courses tend to lead exclusively to academic degrees, people who find the work difficult or falter for any other reason may have a chance of changing subject but they cannot move to an alternative type of course. The scope for change at the new universities is wide. They cater for all kinds of student, from those seeking first-class degrees to students working for professional qualifications by means of part-time courses or evening study.

The polytechnics existed for less than twenty-five years, and in that time they met specific aims. Their libraries are strong on particular course needs, somewhat weaker in more general material. In other ways they may be short

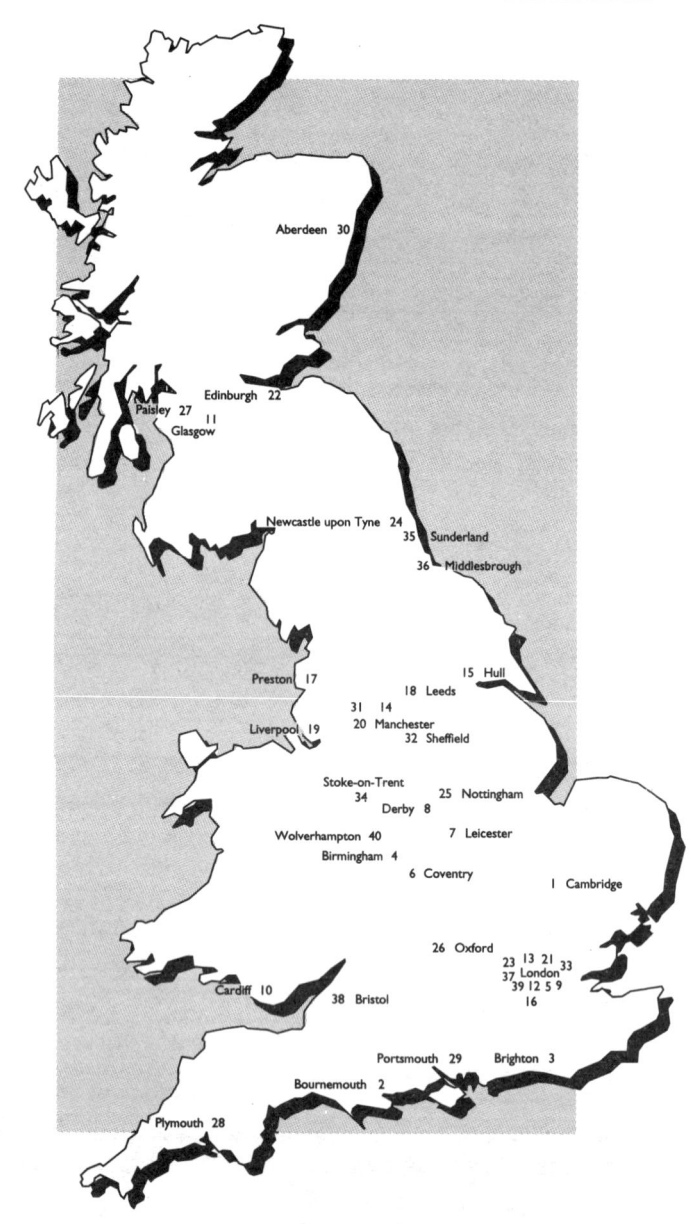

The location of 'new' universities

Key

1. Anglia Polytechnic University
2. Bournemouth University
3. University of Brighton
4. University of Central England in Birmingham
5. London Guildhall University
6. Coventry University
7. De Montfort University
8. Derbyshire University
9. University of East London
10. University of Glamorgan
11. Glasgow Caledonian University
12. University of Greenwich
13. University of Hertfordshire
14. University of Huddersfield
15. University of Humberside
16. Kingston University
17. University of Central Lancashire
18. Leeds Metropolitan University
19. Liverpool John Moores University
20. Manchester Metropolitan University
21. Middlesex University
22. Napier University
23. University of North London
24. University of Northumbria at Newcastle
25. Nottingham Trent University
26. Oxford Brookes University
27. University of Paisley
28. University of Plymouth
29. University of Portsmouth
30. The Robert Gordon University, Aberdeen
31. University College of Salford
32. Sheffield Hallam University
33. South Bank University
34. Staffordshire University
35. University of Sunderland
36. University of Teesside
37. Thames Valley University
38. University of the West of England, Bristol
39. University of Westminster
40. University of Wolverhampton

of assets which have been accumulated in the older universities over generations. Accommodation has often been in rooms privately rented by the student, though halls of residence are on the increase and are quite commonly available for first-year students. Some new universities are spread over many sites and so consist of several inconveniently placed campuses.

This is a list of the new universities.

New name	**Old name**
Anglia Polytechnic University	– Anglia Polytechnic
Bournemouth University	– Bournemouth Polytechnic
University of Brighton	– Brighton Polytechnic
University of Central England in Birmingham	– Birmingham Polytechnic
London Guildhall University	– City of London Polytechnic
Coventry University	– Coventry Polytechnic
De Montfort University	– Leicester Polytechnic
Derbyshire University	– Derbyshire College of Higher Education
University of East London	– Polytechnic of East London
University of Glamorgan	– Polytechnic of Wales
Glasgow Caledonian University	– Glasgow Polytechnic
University of Greenwich	– Thames Polytechnic
University of Hertfordshire	– Hatfield Polytechnic
University of Huddersfield	– The Polytechnic of Huddersfield
University of Humberside	– Humberside Polytechnic
Kingston University	– Kingston Polytechnic
University of Central Lancashire	– Lancashire Polytechnic

Leeds Metropolitan University	– Leeds Polytechnic
Liverpool John Moores University	– The Liverpool Polytechnic
Manchester Metropolitan University	– Manchester Polytechnic
Middlesex University	– Middlesex Polytechnic
Napier University	– Napier Polytechnic of Edinburgh
University of North London	– Polytechnic of North London
University of Northumbria at Newcastle	– Newcastle Polytechnic
Nottingham Trent University	– Nottingham Polytechnic
Oxford Brookes University	– Oxford Polytechnic
University of Paisley	– Paisley College of Technology
University of Plymouth	– Polytechnic South West
University of Portsmouth	– Portsmouth Polytechnic
The Robert Gordon University, Aberdeen	– The Robert Gordon Institute of Technology
University College Salford	– Salford College of Technology
Sheffield Hallam University	– Sheffield City Polytechnic
South Bank University	– South Bank Polytechnic
Staffordshire University	– Staffordshire Polytechnic
University of Sunderland	– Sunderland Polytechnic
University of Teesside	– Teesside Polytechnic
Thames Valley University	– Polytechnic of West London
University of the West of England, Bristol	– Bristol Polytechnic
University of Westminster	– Polytechnic of Central London
University of Wolverhampton	– Wolverhampton Polytechnic

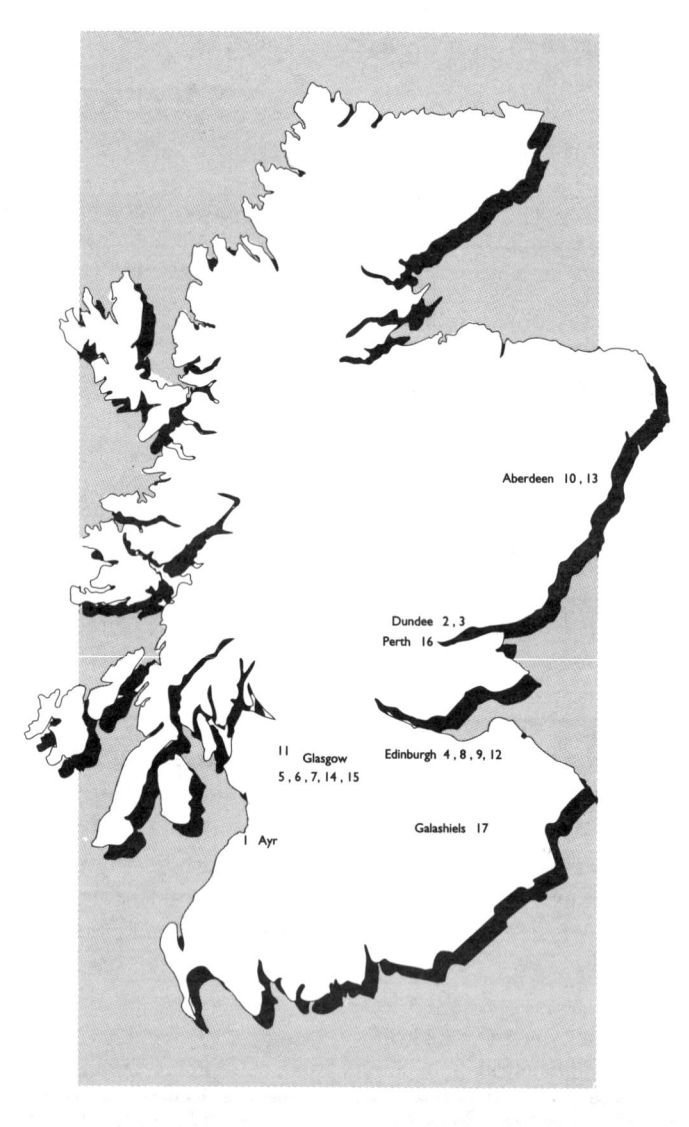

Centrally funded colleges in Scotland

PART 1 • CHOOSING

Scotland

In Scotland, there are older universities, such as Edinburgh and Glasgow, and centrally funded colleges (similar to the former polytechnics). The centrally funded colleges are as follows:

Key

1 Craigie College of Education
2 Duncan of Jordanstone College of Art
3 Dundee Institute of Technology
4 Edinburgh College of Art
5 Glasgow Caledonian University
6 Glasgow School of Art
7 Jordanhill College of Education
8 Moray House Institute of Education
9 Napier University
10 Northern College of Education, Aberdeen
11 University of Paisley
12 Queen Margaret College, Edinburgh
13 The Robert Gordon University, Aberdeen
14 Royal Scottish Academy of Music and Drama
15 St Andrew's College of Education, Glasgow
16 The Scottish Agricultural College, Perth
17 Scottish College of Textiles, Galashiels

The Scottish Agricultural College was formed by the merger of the East of Scotland College of Agriculture, the North of Scotland College of Agriculture and the West of Scotland College of Agriculture. The administrative headquarters of the Scottish Agricultural College are at Perth and the College's sites are at Edinburgh, Aberdeen and Ayr.

Colleges and institutes of higher education

Colleges and institutes of higher education started off as single-discipline institutions, teaching only art, education or another specialist subject. Some of them have now become part of their larger neighbours, the local universities. Others have a special relationship with a local university which validates their degrees. They often preserve the intimate and dedicated atmosphere they had while independent. These colleges are listed in the *UCAS Handbook* and in *The Students' Guide to Higher Education* (see the 'Book List').

Why choose a college or institute of higher education?

Among the reasons given by the colleges are these:

- **BEd courses, which prepare teachers for posts in primary and secondary education, are largely based here (although some universities also provide these courses).**
- **Like universities, colleges and institutes of higher education offer BA and BSc degree courses in humanities and combined studies. These are popular because they allow students to build up a modular or course unit structure, permitting wide flexibility of choice within a large group of arts and science subjects.**
- **Apart from traditional subjects, there are unusual degree or DipHE courses in subjects such as dance, fashion, drama, film and television, sports studies, community studies, etc.**
- **There is a wide range of professional courses in subjects such as building, art and design, management studies, etc.**
- **Many of these courses can be combined with education studies, helping students towards finding**

jobs in education.
- **The colleges have a good reputation academically and for their sound teaching methods.**
- **They are small compared with universities; many are in pleasant rural or town environments and have attractive residential accommodation.**
- **They have a reputation as 'caring' places, providing individual help and assistance, small teaching groups and excellent counselling and careers education services.**
- **They have good sporting, cultural and recreational facilities.**

Further education colleges

Some of these colleges offer degree and higher national diploma courses. They can be grouped as:

- *Colleges of technology*
  - **providing a range of courses in technology, commercial and business subjects**
- *Specialist colleges*
  - **colleges of printing, fashion, building, furniture, art and design, music and technology**
- *General further and higher education colleges*
  - **offering courses ranging from GCSE and A-level, BTEC certificates and diplomas, City and Guilds, and 'Access' courses for mature students, to degrees.**

Consult the CRAC *Directory of Further Education* and write to your local colleges for prospectuses. You may be surprised by the range and quality of the courses offered locally. Entry requirements are the same as for equivalent courses in universities and colleges of higher education, and it is generally easier to get a place.

It is important to remember that different institutions cater for different academic and vocational skills. So choose the one that best suits your needs. The same rule applies within the range of each type of institution. There are hierarchies there too, but you would be well advised to go for the course which suits you and not be swayed by the prestige attached to one institution over another.

Affiliated and Associate Colleges and Franchised Courses

As already mentioned, outside the 96 universities and university colleges there are other colleges that provide first degree courses. They have a special status in relation to a local university which awards their degrees.

Affiliated colleges: their courses are validated by one of the older universities. Examples are Doncaster College (validated by the University of Leeds) and Chester College (by the University of Liverpool). These colleges and their courses are listed in *University and College Entrance, Official Guide*, published by UCAS, and also in *The Students' Guide to Higher Education*, (see the 'Book List').

Associate colleges: they have a special relationship with a former polytechnic, now a university, through which college degree courses are validated. They are listed, with their courses, in CRAC's *Directory of Further Education*.

Franchises: some institutions franchise one, two or more years of a degree or HND course to another, so you may find you study for the first year at a college and then for two years at university, or you take a full course at one college that is validated by a different college or university.

An Eye to a Career

A student intending to join a profession would seem to have little difficulty when making an application to higher education. Vets, architects, doctors, nurses, estate managers and so on require particular qualifications. However, sales representatives, personnel officers, retail managers and advertising account executives are not produced by specialist courses. Huge numbers of graduates every year make career decisions only when they leave college. And a lot of them do jobs like tele-sales for a year until they come up with an idea for a longer-term career. This isn't what we're advising; it may lead to 'if only I'd done X instead' when it's too late.

But you should be aware that if you are stuck for career ideas and do not feel you can narrow your focus at this stage, it will be worth your while to choose a course which does not cut you off from possibilities further down the line. A simple example is GCSE maths. You may have decided never to touch a calculator again when you left school, but how many unrelated courses or jobs have you since discovered for which this is a standard requirement?

Your careers adviser may be able to point out subjects or courses which you should take at college in order to keep open the doors to the kind of careers for which you are now on track. Completing an interest questionnaire will help you to be sure you haven't overlooked careers which you may find of interest.

It is worth actually finding out the minimum qualifications for dream jobs you are vaguely considering. It may be that you won't aim for those qualifications right now, but that at some time in the future a sideways move to another field will make that dream a possibility.

Location of colleges and institutes of higher education to which applications for first degree courses are made through UCAS.

Key

1 Bangor Normal College
2 Bath College of Higher Education
3 Bedford College of Higher Education
4 Bishop Grossteste College, Lincoln
5 Bolton Institute of Higher Education
6 Bradford and Ilkley Community College
7 Bretton Hall College, Wakefield
8 Buckinghamshire College of Higher Education
9 Camborne School of Mines, Cornwall
10 Canterbury Christ College of Higher Education
11 Cardiff Institute of Higher Education
12 Central School of Speech and Drama
13 Charlotte Mason College, Cumbria
14 Cheltenham and Gloucester College of Higher Education
15 Chester College
16 Colchester Institute
17 College of Physiotherapy, Wakefield
18 College of St Mark and St John, Plymouth
19 College of Ripon and York St John, York
20 Crewe and Alsager College of Higher Education
21 Dartington College of Arts, Devon
22 Doncaster College
23 Edge Hill College of Higher Education
24 Falmouth School of Art and Design
25 Farnborough College of Technology
26 Gwent College of Higher Education
27 Harper Adams Agricultural College, Newport, Shropshire
28 Kent Institute of Art and Design
29 King Alfred's College of Higher Education, Winchester
30 La Sainte Union College of Higher Education, Southampton
31 Liverpool Institute of Higher Education
32 The London Institute

33 Luton College of Higher Education
34 Matthew Boulton College, Birmingham
35 Nene College, Northampton
36 New College, Durham
37 Newman and Westhill Colleges, Birmingham
38 North Cheshire College
39 North East Wales Institute of Higher Education
40 North Riding College, Scarborough
41 Norwich City College
42 Ravensbourne College of Design and Communication
43 Roehampton Institute, London
44 St Loye's School of Occupational Therapy, Exeter
45 St Martin's College, Lancaster
46 St Mary's College, Twickenham
47 South Devon College, Torquay
48 Southampton Institute of Higher Education
49 Suffolk College, Ipswich
50 Swansea Institute of Higher Education
51 Trinity and All Saints' College, Leeds
52 Trinity College, Carmarthen
53 University College, Salford
54 Welsh Agricultural College, Aberystwyth
55 Welsh College of Music and Drama, Cardiff
56 West Herts College, Watford
57 West London Institute of Higher Education, Twickenham
58 West Surrey College of Art and Design
59 West Sussex Institute of Higher Education, Bognor Regis
60 Westminster College, Oxford
61 Winchester School of Art
62 Worcester College of Higher Education
63 Writtle College, Essex

How did I end up here?

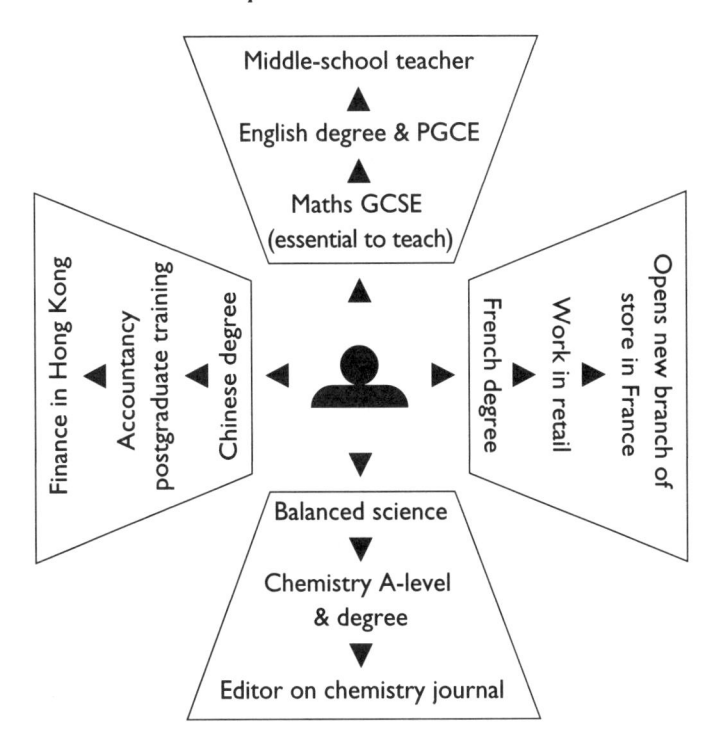

```
                    Middle-school teacher
                            ▲
                    English degree & PGCE
                            ▲
                       Maths GCSE
                    (essential to teach)
                            ▲
  Finance in Hong Kong  ◄  Accountancy postgraduate training  ◄  Chinese degree  ◄  ● ►  French degree  ►  Work in retail  ►  Opens new branch of store in France
                            ▼
                      Balanced science
                            ▼
                     Chemistry A-level
                         & degree
                            ▼
                  Editor on chemistry journal
```

Alternatively, some foundations you lay now may not pay off until your second or third job. It is as well to try and build variety into your study in higher education, to give yourself more than one option when you're choosing a career. Make your base as broad as possible so that you can be flexible. Since you can't predict how your career will develop, make the most of the unexpected by being opportunist – it'll certainly inject some excitement.

Will a degree or diploma help my career?
The answer is obviously yes, but perhaps not in the way you think.

In the first place, by doing a course of higher education, you will gain a new perspective on things. You will acquire knowledge and skills you didn't have before. And you will be trained to think in different ways and have more confidence in putting forward your ideas and opinions. You will be shown how to 'make a case', and this will help you in any job.

It is likely you will change jobs several times during your career. So the better qualified you are at the start, and the more skills you possess, the better prepared you will be for the challenges that come with each change.

Jobs for graduates

A degree or diploma isn't an automatic ticket to a job. It is true that employers look favourably upon graduates. However, graduates need to be *employable* – that is, they need to have vocational skills and demonstrate what employers call the 'right' attitudes: being keen, alert, well motivated and ambitious. You'll have a much better chance in the labour market if you have special knowledge and skills, and a course leading to a degree or diploma will help you get them. And, in a job interview, the person who has some *extra* skills, such as knowledge of a language or of computers, or who can understand business operations, will have a head start, so don't think only in terms of your basic course, but add on special skills – if you can find the time.

There's a very useful little booklet, *First Destinations of University and Polytechnic Graduates*, which gives you some idea of what the traditional graduate jobs are, although the situation changes each year (the booklet is regularly revised). You should also have a look at another book, *What Do Graduates Do?* Once at college, use your college careers service to find out more about jobs and to meet employers.

PART 1 • CHOOSING

With his thesis on marine crustaceans and a copy of GET, *that bible of graduate working opportunities, Edward felt able to face the future with confidence.*

Possible career choices: science and technology

Here are some areas of work to which you could gain entry with a degree or diploma in science and/or technology. Read through it and tick the areas in which you would be interested in working.

- [ ] **Aeronautical engineering**
- [ ] **Agriculture**
- [ ] **Air transport**
- [ ] **Astronomy**
- [ ] **Biochemistry**
- [ ] **Brewing**
- [ ] **Building**
- [ ] **Cartography**
- [ ] **Chemistry**
- [ ] **Chiropody**
- [ ] **Civil engineering**
- [ ] **Computing**
- [ ] **Dentistry**
- [ ] **Dietetics**
- [ ] **Electrical engineering**
- [ ] **Electronics**
- [ ] **Environmental health**

- ☐ Fibre technology
- ☐ Fishing technology
- ☐ Food production
- ☐ Food technology
- ☐ Forestry
- ☐ Fuel technology
- ☐ Geology
- ☐ Glass technology
- ☐ Health science
- ☐ Health-visiting
- ☐ Home economics
- ☐ Horticulture
- ☐ Industrial design
- ☐ Information science
- ☐ Instrument techology
- ☐ Leather technology
- ☐ Mathematics for industry
- ☐ Medical work
- ☐ Metallurgy
- ☐ Meteorology
- ☐ Mineral exploration
- ☐ Mining
- ☐ Mining-surveying
- ☐ Nautical science
- ☐ Naval architecture
- ☐ Nursing
- ☐ Nutrition
- ☐ Ophthalmic optics (optometry)
- ☐ Paint technology
- ☐ Paper and packaging technology
- ☐ Pharmacy
- ☐ Photographic technology
- ☐ Physics
- ☐ Plastics technology
- ☐ Polymer technology
- ☐ Poultry science
- ☐ Printing
- ☐ Psychology
- ☐ Quantity surveying
- ☐ Rubber technology
- ☐ Shipping
- ☐ Statistics
- ☐ Teaching: science and technology
- ☐ Telecommunications
- ☐ Textiles
- ☐ Timber trade
- ☐ Traffic operations
- ☐ Transport
- ☐ Wildlife management
- ☐ Zoology

Possible career choices: arts, business studies, social sciences

For students who are taking arts, business and social science degrees and diplomas, here are some career suggestions.

However, you should be aware that some career choices would require you to have followed a specific course of study, eg town-planning, quantity-surveying, architecture, economics and most design careers. Put ticks in the relevant boxes if you are interested.

- ☐ Accountancy
- ☐ Administration
- ☐ Advertising
- ☐ Archaeology
- ☐ Architecture
- ☐ Art and design
- ☐ Banking
- ☐ Boot and shoe technology
- ☐ Building society work
- ☐ Building surveying work
- ☐ Careers work
- ☐ Catering
- ☐ Child care
- ☐ Church work
- ☐ Civil Service
- ☐ Clerical work
- ☐ Company secretaryship
- ☐ Computer programming
- ☐ Cost control and planning
- ☐ Data-processing
- ☐ Distribution
- ☐ Drama
- ☐ Economics
- ☐ Estate management
- ☐ Estimating
- ☐ Exporting
- ☐ Factory inspection
- ☐ Fashion design
- ☐ Freight forwarding
- ☐ Furniture design
- ☐ Graphic design
- ☐ Home economics
- ☐ Hospital administration
- ☐ Hotel and catering administration
- ☐ Housing management
- ☐ Industrial design
- ☐ Industrial relations
- ☐ Industrial safety
- ☐ Institutional management
- ☐ Insurance
- ☐ Insurance broking
- ☐ Interior design
- ☐ Investment
- ☐ Journalism
- ☐ Land agency
- ☐ Land management
- ☐ Landscape architecture
- ☐ Legal work

- [ ] Librarianship
- [ ] Local government
- [ ] Loss adjusting
- [ ] Management accountancy
- [ ] Management services
- [ ] Market research
- [ ] Marketing
- [ ] Medical social work
- [ ] Merchandising
- [ ] Military careers
- [ ] Nursing
- [ ] Occupational therapy
- [ ] Organisation and methods
- [ ] Orthoptics
- [ ] Park administration
- [ ] Personnel work
- [ ] Photography
- [ ] Physiotherapy
- [ ] Piloting (air)
- [ ] Police work
- [ ] Probation work
- [ ] Psychiatric social work
- [ ] Public relations
- [ ] Purchasing
- [ ] Quantity surveying
- [ ] Radiography
- [ ] Rating and valuation-surveying
- [ ] Reinsurance
- [ ] Retail management
- [ ] Seamanship
- [ ] Secretarial work
- [ ] Selling and sales administration
- [ ] Social work
- [ ] Speech therapy
- [ ] Stock exchange work
- [ ] Surveying: land, general
- [ ] Systems analysis
- [ ] Teaching: arts, business studies, social sciences
- [ ] Textile design
- [ ] Town and country-planning
- [ ] Transport work
- [ ] Welfare work
- [ ] Youth work

Where College Meets Work: Sandwich Courses

Students considering careers connected with science, engineering and some social sciences have the option of taking a sandwich course. 'Sandwich' refers to the periods of work in industry sandwiched between your periods at college.

When Shibani returned from her first industrial placement, the girls noticed a change in her.

You will hear of thick and thin sandwich courses. A *thick* sandwich begins with one or two years in college, usually followed by a full year in industry, finishing with a final year in education.

A *thin* sandwich is made up of several periods of industrial experience. Usually, each of the first three years of the course is divided between academic work and experience in industry, commerce or business, with the fourth and final year spent entirely in college.

When you take a sandwich degree course at a college or university, you can expect the institution to make some, or most, of the arrangements for training, and you can be given a range of experiences with different employers. However, in a period of economic recession, it is very difficult to place students in companies and you may be expected to help find your own placement. At your application interview you should ask who bears the responsibility for finding placements.

Furthermore, because of the difficulty of finding training places in companies, you may find that your course changes from a sandwich to a full-time course.

The main characteristics of sandwich courses are listed below.

- **Courses generally last a year longer than equivalent full-time degree or higher national courses (that is, four years rather than three years).**
- **They are usually in subjects closely linked to industry, particularly engineering, technology and the sciences (although there are some social science sandwich courses such as law and geography).**
- **Academic study alternates with one or more periods of industrial experience.**
- **Industrial experience can range from three to twelve months.**
- **Training and work experience are supervised by college and company staff.**

A sandwich course can add valuable experience to your academic cv. Remember that employers look for other qualities apart from an applicant's academic record. They look for evidence that a graduate will fit into their company or organisation, will be able to work with people in a team and is capable of solving problems. It is a real bonus to take a course that develops your interpersonal and communication skills, and your familiarity with the business environment as well as developing your academic knowledge and skills.

Is a sandwich course right for you?

Here are some statements to which you should be able to answer 'yes' if you're a likely candidate for a sandwich course.

I am a practical person.
I like to apply ideas and knowledge to working situations.
I enjoy working in a team.
I want my education to prepare the ground for a career I have already singled out for myself.
I want to start work before I qualify.
I'd like to sort out where I'm going in work fairly soon.
I like variety.
I like being on the move.
I settle quickly into different environments.
I need a break from college work.
I have clear career objectives.
I prefer a course with a vocational emphasis.

On the other hand, how do you rate the items below? If the following are important to you, you are probably a candidate for another kind of course.

I don't need to relate my studies to possible future employment to enjoy them.
I'm happy leaving ideas about careers after college until later.
My course isn't available in a sandwich.
I'm interested in areas of work other than business – broadcasting, teaching, archaeology, medicine, etc.
I think a three-year degree course is long enough.

Looking for Sponsorship? A Way to Pay for College

The whole issue of who's paying for your higher education is dealt with in detail in Part 3. However, as sponsorship may affect your choice of course and institution, it's mentioned here as well.

Sponsorship means that a company which plans to employ you when you graduate will pay you a bursary while you study. Exactly how much varies. Usually, you are expected to work for the sponsor during your vacations, or during the placements of your sandwich course. You may be entitled to a full salary while you study, as well as a bursary which can vary between £300 and £2,000 a year. Sponsors are keen to fund students on vocational courses, particularly in science, technology, engineering and business studies.

Begin your investigation of this area by reading *Students and Sponsorship 1994*. Over two hundred companies, the Armed Forces, public corporations and nationalised industries offer sponsorships. They are listed, together with the benefits they provide, in *The Which? Guide to Sponsorship in Higher Education*.

To apply for sponsorship, consult the reference sources mentioned in the 'Book List' and write to at least ten companies or organisations. In general, you should start approaching companies for sponsorship twelve months to two years before you intend starting your HE course. If the company is interested in you, you will be invited for interview. Some industry-sponsored sandwich courses differ from those described earlier. They are often in the pattern 1:3:1; that is, one year with the sponsor, three years in full-time education, then another year with the sponsor. The *Which?* guide mentioned above also lists the *courses* that carry or offer student sponsorship. You can thus find out which *courses* carry sponsorship for each *subject* in a particular institution. Universities have arrangements with companies by which training places are offered as part of a wider arrangement in which research, staff and projects also attract sponsorship.

Professional and Vocational Courses

Professional courses are offered at most colleges and universities. They lead to, or give exemption from, the examinations of professional institutions in areas such as law, banking, personnel management, and engineering.

To find out about professional courses and qualifications, you should write to the institution of the profession in which you are interested and ask for details. You will find the addresses of these professional bodies in careers books and libraries.

Vocational courses are those which lead to a qualification with direct relevance to a job. Courses in construction, engineering, business studies, advertising, accounting, journalism and many others come into this category. To find out where such courses are offered, consult CRAC's *Directory of Higher Education*, or ask at your local technical college, college of technology or college of further education. Entry levels can vary from two A-levels or the equivalent (for advanced courses) to two to four GCSE subjects, passed at grades A to C. Another way into a professional or vocational career is to take a degree in the relevant subject. The degree will give you exemption from all or part of the exams set by the professional body. To find out about degree courses, consult *University and College Entrance – The Official Guide* and the ECCTIS database.

A Year Abroad – Studying

Some courses allow a student to spend a year or more in an institution overseas, usually within Europe but possibly in the USA or elsewhere. Students taking foreign language courses usually spend up to a year studying or working in the country whose language they are studying. But in recent years this option has been extended to engineering, business studies and many other degree and HND courses. Some of the pioneers

Nigel sensed that his year in Vladivostok would hold a dear place in his memory.

in this development were Sussex University and Middlesex University. These courses are called joint-study courses. You will find details in course prospectuses.

If studying abroad appeals to you, you should check out the opportunities to undertake a degree or diploma at a foreign institution. You are able to apply direct to *any* higher education institution. However, obtaining a grant is likely to be difficult. Most full-time students who study abroad are paid for privately, but you should keep a lookout for special funds and projects designed to encourage cordial foreign relations. For example, under a scheme called the European Community Action Scheme for the Mobility of University Students – ERASMUS for short – grants are available for students to study for part of their UK degree or diploma course in another European Community country. What is more, ERASMUS has organised a scheme allowing institutions to give credits to students who have completed a period of study in an overseas institution. This arrangement is very attractive to UK students because it means they qualify for UK awards and grants, and can study in Europe, perhaps obtaining a dual qualification from two institutions.

There are two other European initiatives – LINGUA and COMETT. They confine themselves respectively to the disciplines of language-training and technology. Courses that incorporate them have a distinct bonus. As world communications continue to improve there is likely to be a growth in shared or joint courses.

Qualifications to Choose Between
Degrees and diplomas

Essentially a degree or HND is an honour conferred (despite the fact that it is often said to have been 'taken') on a student in recognition of a completed course of study.

First degrees usually lead to the award of a bachelor degree, either an honours degree or a pass (or ordinary) degree. Honours degrees are the more difficult. They are usually graded first, second (with upper second and lower second) and third. A pass degree is sometimes awarded if a student does not reach the standard expected of an honours candidate. For instance, if examination marks during a three or four-year course are not good enough to justify going on with an honours course, a student may be offered the chance to work for an ordinary degree. The letters after your name at the end will not have the (Hons) addition as in BA (Hons) or BSc (Hons). It is worth knowing that most employers prefer honours graduates.

Diploma of Higher Education

The Diploma of Higher Education is a two-year programme of work across several subjects chosen from a wide selection of options and is designed to provide advanced study for people who do not yet want to specialise in one particular area.

These courses are offered at some universities and colleges of higher education. The entry level for the diploma is the same as the general requirement for a degree course – two A-levels.

After two years, students may receive the DipHE or transfer to a BSc or BA degree which takes a further two years to complete. Another option is to transfer to a BEd degree course and gain a teaching qualification.

The DipHE is fully established, but it is essential to make sure that the university or college in which you are interested has options 'end-on' to the DipHE; that is, degree courses to which you can transfer after two years. Some DipHEs, you will see, are designed as two-year courses in their own right.

Students say that the advantage of a DipHE course is that it delays the choice of deciding on the final degree course until several alternatives have been tried.

DipHE courses qualify for grants in the same way as degree courses, so you won't be at any kind of financial disadvantage if you choose to take the course. You should, however, check the grant position with your LEA if you want to go beyond the DipHE.

BTEC and SCOTVEC

The Business and Technology Education Council (BTEC) and

The Scottish Vocational Education Council (SCOTVEC) approve vocational courses run by colleges, schools and universities. The BTEC and SCOTVEC programmes cover an extremely wide range of subjects including agriculture, business and finance, caring, computing, construction, design, distribution, engineering, hotel and catering, leisure and science. If you have a vocation in mind, there's likely to be a relevant BTEC course.

Awards are at three main levels – first, national and higher national. A-level students would normally apply to do higher national level courses. The Higher National Diploma takes two or three years full-time or three years part-time. The Higher National Certificate takes two years part-time. Holders of a BTEC national certificate or national diploma are qualified to study for a degree or HND, if they have the grades required by universities. BTEC higher national programmes are available at universities, colleges of higher education and FE colleges.

The courses are closely related to what you need to know for jobs in business. Among the companies and organisations that like people to have BTEC qualifications are:

- **manufacturing companies**
- **engineering firms**
- **insurance offices**
- **building societies**
- **banks**
- **personnel departments**
- **shops and supermarkets**
- **the police**
- **the Civil Service**
- **hospital administration**
- **transport companies**
- **travel agencies**

- **food companies**
- **food offices.**

On these courses you can learn:
- **how businesses are organised**
- **how to deal with various business problems**
- **office administration**
- **money matters**
- **how to work with people in a team**
- **how to communicate clearly on the telephone, in writing, etc**
- **how to make the best use of your abilities and skills.**

College diplomas and certificates

Most further education colleges, institutes and colleges of higher education and universities have their own diploma or certificate courses. Among the courses carrying these qualifications you will find advertising, art and design, communications studies, computer studies, drama, languages, music and many more.

Some of the courses give exemption from the examinations of professional bodies, as in accountancy, law, personnel management, building, engineering and estate management.

How Long Does HE Take? ....

Courses vary in length from two to five years.

The usual length of a first degree course is three years in England and Wales and four in Scotland. Some language courses include a year abroad which therefore extends the course by another year. Some social science courses, like the one at Bath University, are four years. Applied science and technology degree courses of the sandwich type (that is, with industrial training in companies or organisations) are usually four years. Vocational degree courses in subjects such as architecture, dentistry, medicine, and veterinary science may be four or five years. Higher national diploma (HND) courses are two years full-time or three years part-time.

Course Comparisons: Six Important Points

As you narrow down your choice of institution, you should note that few teach the same subject in exactly the same way. Here are some points to think about as you make your choice of degree or diploma course.

Courses of the same name at different institutions may have much less in common than you would expect.

When the staff of a teaching department select material for a course lasting three or four years, they can choose from a tremendous body of knowledge and skills in their subject. They are likely to give priority to those topics they consider offer the greatest understanding of the subject and they will inevitably be influenced by their own interests and research experience in the subject. So don't expect courses of the same name to be exactly the same in content. As an example, a history course can be mostly medieval history at one place and at another be mainly concerned with the history of the last 200 years. This applies to any course.

Some courses may have a compulsory element; others may offer options; others can offer the chance to combine subjects. You will find courses that encourage early specialisation in particular areas.

In other instances, you will find courses with very different names bearing remarkable similarities. Bristol University's modern languages, for instance, shares many features with Coventry's European studies degree. Extracts from course descriptions, on page 71, illustrate this point.

One way to tackle this problem is to consult the ECCTIS database. It carries summaries of each course in every university and college. Refer, too, to *Hobsons' Degree Course Guides* and *Which Degree?* (see the 'Book List') for information about different subjects.

Having picked out, say, half a dozen possibilities, send away for the prospectuses of the departments you have selected. If you do this homework before going for interview, you will make a very good initial impression on the interviewer.

There are sometimes subsidiary subjects which you have to do along with a main subject.

Bristol's modern languages course, illustrated in the extracts, includes a foundation course in social sciences. The inclusion of, say, statistics in a maths course could be enough to decide you for or against the course.

Admissions tutors will expect you to know something about compulsory topics or subjects in the course, and to have some idea of the options available. You can get this information from the department or course syllabus. Options are courses within the degree or diploma which may last a term, a year or longer. You are given a range to choose from, and you work through your chosen option until you complete it and are free to replace it with another option from a fresh list of choices. So in a course on, say, biology, there will be some compulsory

BRISTOL
Modern Languages BA (Hons)
Full-time; 4 years
Special requirements: 2 'A' levels from French, German, Spanish or 1 'A' level from French, German, Spanish and other acceptable 'A' level pass(es) for applicant to be admitted to the intensive beginners course in Spanish or German. GCSE/'O' level pass in English Language and Mathematics. Mature applicants or those holding 'AS' levels in a language will be admitted on the basis of an interview.

Curriculum
The course provides the study of two foreign languages (from French, German and Spanish) and three Social Sciences - History, Politics and Economics. From Year 2 students opt for one of these 3 Social Science subjects. Equal weighting is given to each language throughout. A complementary course in Linguistics seeks to give students the theoretical background of the foreign languages.
Year 1/2 - Studies include Contemporary Studies of relevant countries. Translation, composition, comprehension, oral communication and interpreting are taught in the Applied Language courses. There is a Social Science Foundation Course in Year 1, followed by a choice of History, Politics or Economics in Year 2.
Year 3 - Students spend two consecutive five-month periods abroad. They will normally work in industry or as an assistant in a school, but may opt for approved courses of study. During Year 3 two project dissertations are written.
Year 4 is characterised by specialisation and choice. In Applied Language students specialise in translating and interpreting whilst in Social Science they have a choice between International Economic Relationships, Comparative Politics and National Crisis in Western Europe 1929–40. Linguistics offers courses in Critique of Translation and Natural Language Processing, Machine Translation. Portuguese, Italian and Dutch are offered to students of Spanish, French and German respectively. For students of exceptional calibre an Erasmus stream is available which allows students to spend two full academic years in two countries.

COVENTRY
European Studies BA & BA (Hons), DipHE
Full-time; 4 years
Curriculum
The course offers a programme of study which combines a main Language (French, German and Spanish) with courses in Politics, History and International Relations, and contains specific integrating elements, relating to the development of the European Community. Students spend the third year of the course in the country of their main language, undertaking a programme of specified education and training. Whilst the main geographical focus is on the countries of the European Community, options are available which deal with Eastern Europe, European-American relations, and a wide range of other topics.

subjects, and perhaps options to take genetics, bacteriology or microbial ecology. There are usually more options available as courses proceed; there may be few options at the start.

The opportunity to change courses after you have arrived varies from institution to institution.

Not all establishments allow it, but most are flexible. The need comes about for different reasons. In the first place, many courses have a general first year involving the study of related 'minor' or 'subsidiary' subjects. Occasionally, students become so interested in one of these that they ask to transfer to that subject. Other students ask to make a complete switch from, say, law to English, or physics to engineering, as they simply feel they are not on the right course for them. You should find out from a prospectus or interview how requests to transfer are regarded. It will depend partly on your academic qualifications. But you will probably find that such requests, as long as they are backed up with good arguments and strong feelings, are sympathetically received.

Switches or transfers are best done before the end of the first year; after that it becomes more difficult to change direction, not least because of grant regulations.

Candidates with A-level grades too low to be acceptable for the subjects they want to study have sometimes turned tactical, applied for and have been accepted on courses for which there is less competition, and switched courses at the end of their first term or year. You too may find this works, but the authorities may be perfectly aware of the trick and discourage the change.

A final word of caution: make sure that any subject you are likely to want to switch to is available at your college.

Changing one's course was obviously not encouraged.

Subjects with the most widespread appeal attract the largest number of applicants.

Those with limited appeal obviously attract the fewest. The moral to be drawn from this is that you may want to weigh up your grades against the popularity of the subject you are considering, to decide how promising your chances of acceptance look. The other point is that if your chosen course has a lot of vacancies, should you be asking why it's not popular? Obviously, the best policy is to acquire as much information as possible from books, prospectuses and students.

Understand the differences between the meanings of 'pure' and 'applied' and go for the one that suits you.

A pure science course will lean towards theoretical and academic studies. Applied means that knowledge is slanted towards a manufacturing, engineering or other technological process. Some examples of applied subjects are: control engineering, fuel technology, paper science, photography, glass technology and textile technology.

In arts subjects it is as well to be aware that some have a literary slant while others comprise, say, language courses which may give training for a career in translating or interpreting. Applied language courses are likely to emphasise the social, political and economic aspects of a country rather than its literature.

A Word about Art and Design Courses

These courses can be taken at specialist colleges, in further education colleges and some universities. If you are planning to take a degree course or a BTEC HND course in art and design or in media, you should send your application to the Art and Design Admissions Registry (ADAR) between early February and the end of March. You are allowed a choice of two institutions.

Some colleges have their own certificates and diplomas, but others prepare students for BTEC examinations in the following areas of art and design:

- **Graphics**   Advertising design, photography, media design, books and magazine design, film and television.

- **Textiles and fashion**   Printed, woven and knitted textiles, plastics, wallpapers.

- **Three-dimensional design**   Industrial design, display and exhibition, interior design, furniture, jewellery, silversmithing, glass, theatre design.

Teaching and Learning: Structures and Styles
Course structures

When you move to any institution of higher education, responsibility for your progress rests more or less squarely on your shoulders. You have to arrange your own timetable to take in lectures, private or library work, and time spent in lab, studio or workshop. There is no compulsion to sit in formal classes as there was at school. The number of occasions on which your presence would be missed by the authorities are few.

The main differences between studying at 16+ and undergraduate work are:

- **Contact hours**   There is less formal teaching in higher education. The amount of time spent sitting in class is less than at school.
- **Private study**   In higher education the responsibility for organising work passes completely to the student. You will be expected to arrange your own timetable.
- **Freedom**   This is the freedom to plan your work. It can be heady and exciting, for there is a lot of it, but don't abuse it by failing to complete your workload.

- **Self-organisation**   The consequence of freedom is the need to arrange your own working timetable, mixing private study with practical assignments, and not forgetting social, sporting, cultural and recreational activities.
- **Study skills**   You should have learned some study skills during your A-level study: how to organise your time, how to use the library, how to take notes and so on. You will have to sharpen and extend these skills when you are on your own.
- **The workload**   This is considerable and should not be underestimated. Not everyone is able to adapt to the changes and it may take you time to adjust. However, you can make life as easy as possible for yourself by taking account of the different ways in which the courses you have chosen are structured and of the learning and teaching styles they involve.

Programmes of work leading to a degree are constructed in various ways. The main structures are as follows:

Single-subject courses

On these courses you concentrate on just one subject – music, biochemistry or whatever. However, although most of your work will be focused on this subject, you may find that there are optional or subsidiary subjects to be taken as well. For instance, a single-subject history course would possibly cover a wide area from prehistory to the modern day, and also include subsidiary courses in politics, government, philosophy and economics. These may seem like diversions from your chief interest but they are designed to broaden your understanding of your subject and its context, and often lead students into completely new lines of study and personal interest. Another kind of single-subject course is one where two or three subjects are studied in the first year before students move on to the study of a single subject in the second and third years. These are quite common, and are often marked by 'Part one' and 'Part two' divisions, corresponding to the first and then the second/third years.

Joint courses

In this kind of course two or more single subjects are joined together so that you take a degree in, say, English and history, or economics and accounting, or physics and geography or two foreign languages. You don't do twice as much work as in a single subject, but take about 50 per cent from each course.

Combined courses

On a combined studies course the student selects from a group of subjects to make up his or her individual course. A fairly common example is a combined sciences course where several science subjects are taken during the first year, and two or three are studied in more detail in the second and third years of the course. The University of Hertfordshire, for example, has a BSc combined sciences course which includes astronomy, business, chemistry, economics, applied physics, human biology, a choice of three languages and psychology. In a BA humanities course, a programme can be constructed from subjects such as English, languages, music, psychology and philosophy. You may find a three or four-year course divides into major subjects – studied for a longer time and in more detail – and minor subjects, taken for only a year. Minor subjects are also called subsidiary or ancillary subjects.

Modular courses

There are a number of variations within modular courses, but the main point is that this type of course is divided into 'modules' or sections, which are taught and examined separately, without final examinations. Oxford Brookes University pioneered modular courses and there is now (as at other institutions) a 'menu' of modules from which students can choose combinations as long as the modules can be timetabled without clashes. A single module in this case is a unit of study of about one hundred hours, but this differs elsewhere. A full-time honours student may be expected to pass the equivalent of three or four modules in a term, and build up a total package of 20 or 30 modules over a three-year course.

Harriet's thirst for knowledge knew no bounds. The thought of dropping her beloved subjects for a single honours was too much. No, she must take a modular course.

Interdisciplinary degree courses

A phrase occasionally used in prospectuses is 'interdisciplinary study'. A 'discipline' is very close to what we have been calling a subject. These new courses have broken down traditional subject divisions in order to give students the opportunity to study areas across a whole range of subjects, rather like the combined courses. On an interdisciplinary course each 'subject' is divided up into courses of a standard length and similar workload, and a full degree programme is built up from these units. In effect, then, you can build up a total course covering a number of subjects – for instance, English, psychology, politics, and so on.

Teaching and learning styles

Just as structures vary, so do the learning situations you will encounter. You may have experienced tutorials and lectures at your sixth-form college. You will read about them and other modes of teaching and learning in prospectuses. It is as well to be aware of them, and what they demand of you, so that you can distinguish between your short-listed courses by judging how well you will adapt to the teaching styles they each involve.

Those listed below are the most common. Most courses involve a combination of these teaching styles. You should look out for the balance which suits you best.

Lectures

In most institutions a lecture is usually a one-hour period cut by five minutes or so at each end to allow students to assemble and depart. You may be one of a hundred students sitting in a tiered lecture theatre, feeling overawed by the scale of the gathering, or pleasantly anonymous in the crowd, or you may be one of only half a dozen students and be known personally by the lecturer. In either case you will be expected to absorb spoken information and take your own detailed notes.

Attendance at lectures may be voluntary, but only foolish students are consistently absent. Some lecturers base their end-of-term or end-of-year exams on their lecture material. Others use lectures as a means of guiding students through work related to assignments. Some lectures are so stimulating and amusing that to miss them is to miss a great experience. Lectures delivered by academics who have thought about and studied a subject in great depth for many years are not to be missed for their quality. On the other hand, lectures can be dull, boring, and may seem to you to be irrelevant to your work. It is strongly advised, however, that lectures should be attended regularly, given the exceptions of occasional lapses and absences.

You will find your own solution to the question of how best to record the lectures you attend. Some students do not take notes. They listen and absorb, and maybe write up their ideas afterwards. Others find they need to make brief notes of headings, references, ideas and judgments. Others write at a furious pace. Others again neither listen nor write. You will work out your own response, and you may discuss it with other students. But remember that for some lecturers and some courses, lectures are the chief means of dispensing information and ideas, and for many students they are the main route to understanding a topic or a subject.

How many lectures will there be in a week? This is impossible to answer. In science, the average seems to be about 12 in a week (with another 12 hours' practical work), but in technological subjects the total may well be higher. In arts subjects, the lecture load varies from the light (six or eight hours a week) to 10 or 12; in all cases additional time is needed for reading and preparation.

Tutorials

Like lectures, tutorials differ from place to place. However, it can be said that there are two kinds:

1. **A one-to-one interview, discussion or talk with a lecturer who is a course tutor. Here you will discuss some aspect of your work – an exam paper, an essay, some reading, a project, an experiment, your work in the lab, workshop or studio. A tutorial such as this can last anything from 20 minutes to over an hour.**
2. **Two or three students join a tutor to read a piece of their work – an essay or analysis – or discuss an item or topic which has been prepared by one or more students in the group. In this small group you will be expected to contribute to a general discussion.**

Seminars

This method of teaching is particularly common in arts departments. A group of students, numbering anything from a few to a dozen, works with at least one lecturer – perhaps two or three. Generally, notice is given of a topic to be discussed and everyone will do some preliminary work – reading, or practical work in the lab or studio – designed to ferret out ideas or information to be brought to the meeting. The lecturer will usually introduce the topic and then everyone will be expected to contribute to a round-table discussion. Sometimes, a student will be expected to make a presentation. If seminars are to be a part of your course, get in some practice.

Workshops, labs and studios

Students who take practically based subjects, such as art and design, photography, technology, science or architecture, will be expected to put in a lot of time in workshops, studios or laboratories, often unsupervised by teaching staff. There is no set amount, but on average about 10 hours a week should be spent on practical work.

Time rolled back when Sunil visited the professor to discuss the works of Pope, Keats, Marvell...

Audio-visual teaching

Some lecturers are keen on using audio-visual equipment to teach. This may include an overhead projector, or slides, or tape-slides, or a video. Most HE institutions are well equipped with language laboratories, closed-circuit television and lecture rooms equipped with audio-visual aids. However, teaching methods using audio-visual aids have not yet caught on in the way that enthusiasts expected, and you will find that the use of these aids will vary. Only the Open University, with its system of distance learning via the telephone, by post, and by means of radio and television, has really adapted to electronic support and made a real success of it. You will generally find that older teaching methods – by lecture, tutorial and seminar – still dominate. However, good lecturers use a variety of teaching aids, including the overhead projector, flip-charts, the blackboard, slides and videos.

Private study

In addition to coursework in lecture halls, rooms and labs, students are expected to work on their own. People taking arts subjects, for example, can expect two to three hours of lectures a day, plus occasional tutorials. The rest of their study time will be spent on their own. In order to complete essays, prepare discussion topics, assemble projects and complete other course work, a lot of time has to be spent in libraries, hunting out books and references, and in the privacy of one's own room studying. Most course tutors give students a reading list, which they are expected to work their way through. Time is also needed to write up experiments or projects completed in labs and workshops.

Methods of Assessment

Again, this is an area in which you will find alternative styles and probably one particular type that you prefer. Course prospectuses are the place to look for information on assessment.

Examination

Some courses have exams at regular – and frequent – intervals. Others are spaced out more kindly. Whatever the form, exams will decide your progress. They are generally of the three-hour type, similar to A-level exams. However, departments often impose other hurdles, such as tests or shorter exams, to determine a student's progress. Medical and veterinary science students often have *vivas* as part of the assessment. These are oral exams lasting anywhere between ten to thirty minutes in which you will be quizzed by a panel of examiners.

Continuous assessment

Some institutions and departments have devised systems of assessment whereby all your coursework – essays, projects, lab and studio work, portfolio presentations, experimental work, etc – is taken into account in a yearly assessment which counts towards your final degree award.

Even where continuous assessment is used, the way it is used varies enormously. Some courses have up to 80 per cent continuous assessment; in others the percentage is much lower.

Non-academic Criteria ··························

The choices presented by the alternatives already discussed may seem to you to be the only ones of any importance. The choices that follow are secondary considerations to your choice of place and subject and the academic variations on offer, but may influence your happiness a great deal.

Moving to college may cause far-reaching changes that you aren't expecting; coping with new responsibilities in a new environment may give you another perspective on yourself and your relations with others. For students who do have problems of adjustment while at college, there are supportive welfare and counselling services, and almost every university and college has a 'nightline' and other kinds of assistance to help students in difficulty.

Only you can decide how congenial you find an environment, but any place will affect how you feel. The important thing is to be reasonably certain that when you embark on higher education you are not going to find yourself allergic to some aspect of your surroundings. A glance through the following points may remind you to check on things that could make or mar the next few years, and make your choices accordingly.

Size

This refers to many of the new factors to which you will be adapting: size of town or city, the size of the college, of your department, hall of residence, and so on. You might love the busy city life of Manchester or London or Liverpool; but it is worth remembering that it could be costly to take full advantage of what the city offers – daily fares to and from college alone can be expensive. The institution itself may have anything from a few hundred to ten thousand or more students. The one may be friendly and intimate, the other vast and impersonal. On the other hand the smaller place may have fewer facilities of all kinds, may seem parochial or complacent or staid, and is less likely to allow changes in course or tutors if the first choice proves unsatisfactory. The size of a college will be indicated in its prospectus, though colleges invariably see their own as utopian.

Environment

The new universities tend to be in urban settings. The older universities and other colleges may be in the middle of cities, or set in grassy downland, or somewhere in between. The centre of a town may offer much in the way of culture, entertainment and social life. A suburb may provide none of these, and access to the city centre may be limited. It may on the other hand offer easy access (by public transport, or bicycle, or foot) to beautiful countryside.

It may be important to check out public transport, especially if you plan to make frequent visits to home or distant friends. There are places where a good cheap bus service makes it possible to go from a rural college to a lively town centre and return within an evening, but it's unlikely that the service will continue into the early hours. You might end up paying for a taxi!

England, Northern Ireland, Scotland, Wales

Each country in the UK has its own heritage and identity. You may be attracted by the idea of studying and living in a country you do not know; for ancestral reasons perhaps, or simple intuition, scenery, or the closeness of the sea. But bear in mind that the more remote you are from your home, the more money is likely to be eaten up by travel tickets.

Social criteria

How significant do you feel these criteria are for you?

- **Opportunities for entertainment, meeting people, night life and so on, both on the campus and in the neighbouring town.**
- **Ratio of males to females. You might be of the opinion that equal numbers make for the best atmosphere. Bear in mind that a large majority of one over the other may affect the character of the place.**
- **Boyfriend or girlfriend. It has been the experience of many that going to the same institution as their boy or girlfriend from home was a bad idea. It may be more difficult to make friends if you are thought of as part of a couple: you may appear self-sufficient and intimidating to single students; party-givers like the unattached; jealousy may raise its head; life could become a bit middle-aged. Meeting your boy or girlfriend at weekends only, when you have chosen separate colleges, can give you the best of both worlds.**

Cultural thoughts

With student travel and entrance reductions and a flexible timetable, being a student can be a real bonus if you want to take advantage of the cultural activities on and off the campus.

Find out what's available in terms of cinema, theatre, dance, concerts, etc. On the other hand, lower standards of what is currently available may be what you're looking for if you intend to initiate one or other of these activities yourself, and want to make a mark.

Unpleasant though it may have been, Cheryl was later to see the 'rat incident' as formative in her rise to power in the students' union.

Students' unions

Across the country there are students' unions of all shapes, sizes, vices and virtues. They offer all kinds of personal help to students in distress or crisis. Some put most of their energy into politics, dissent and protest. Most take seriously the various aspects of student life such as health care, welfare, transport, and entertainment. Others are much less active on behalf of the student body. The unions are run by students for students and are a wonderful starting ground for fledgling public speakers, politicians, organisers, treasurers, journalists and so on. If you think you'd like to get your cv off to a flying start, then find a union with lots of get up and go and take an active part in its life.

Sport

Athletes of a high standard for whom their sport is an abiding passion will not need to be told to check that the facilities exist at the standards they require (plenty of colleges provide facilities up to and above county standard; some none at all). They will know to enquire about the training on offer, and how good the trainers are.

Even if you have no specific plans to take up a sport, it is worth checking out the facilities, as plenty of students who have never played games or participated in athletics or team sports discover at college a sport they like, because here, for the first time, are cheap accessible squash courts or a swimming pool or whatever. Some of the colleges and universities in towns offer wonderful chances to see great teams or individuals in play.

More cultural thoughts

It would be misleading not to mention class, snobbery, inverted snobbery, public and state schools, vast differentials in personal wealth, and so on. Institutions attract differing proportions of public school and state school students. If this is of any importance to you, it is as well to find out about the student intake statistics before you visit. Spending a trip finding out that this sort of consideration removes the place from your options is not as constructive as a journey which decides you in favour of an institution!

The prestige or reputation of a college or department is not always a very reliable indicator of its value to you. The giants and geniuses who create reputations move on to other appointments and may leave few traces behind. They may be more famous for research than teaching, and are not likely to come in touch with first-year students anyway. So a reputation needs to be accompanied by more solid testimonials. A steady output of graduates who in time became distinguished may be a better indicator; though it is not unknown for a place of education to rest on its distant past.

Disabled Students
Getting information

A good contact to know is SKILL. This organisation has up-to-date information on the facilities in all establishments of higher education in the country. Look for a section in the official prospectuses of the places you are applying to that explains any procedures specifically designed for your application.

If there is no mention, write to the registrar or secretary, indicating the course or courses in which you are interested, and explain the nature of your disability, whether mental or physical. It might be something they can accommodate, but it is always best to keep them informed. The point made by all institutions is that they must know about a disability before a student joins a course, not on the date the student arrives. Then, if you are offered a place, the university or college will address your particular needs. Sometimes use is made of Community Service Volunteers.

Applications are taken on merit, and students who have had behavioural problems at school or at home often find that a new environment for both living and learning can be immensely helpful.

Accommodation

Some places provide special accommodation for physically

handicapped students – ground-floor rooms and flats, special lifts and so on. As soon as you are offered a place, write to the accommodation officer describing your disability.

Mature Students

'Mature students' are technically those aged 21 and over at the start of their course. The number of mature students in higher education is likely to grow as the notion of 'second chance' and 'life-long educational opportunity' takes hold in a society with increased leisure time. The criteria on which the mature student bases her/his choice will, of course, include many of the foregoing, but probably overriding them all will be the mature student's personal circumstances: location, spouse, children, and work commitments. Funding is another important issue.

Access courses

Many local colleges of further education now offer Access courses. These teach mature students how to use libraries and reference material, how to take notes, plan and organise study, how to construct and write essays, and how to improve their concentration. These courses are linked to and built around a syllabus in a particular subject such as design, science or a vocational subject. Access courses are designed to help mature students without formal academic qualifications to enter higher education and this qualification is recognised as an alternative to A-levels.

The best available

Institutions vary in the way they consider mature applicants, but most respond favourably. Most officially require evidence of recent study (for example, the preparatory courses offered by colleges of further education), and will take professional or occupational qualifications or experience into account.

A few, notably Birkbeck College and Goldsmiths' College in London, offer part-time degree courses and will accept mature students without qualifications on paper, provided they have other qualifications or can show evidence of academic potential. Some of the new universities have gone further. For example, London Guildhall University offers modular degree courses which allow mature students to combine parts of different courses into one qualification. Most universities offer nursery facilities to student parents, shortened day courses (10 am to 3 pm) and an associate student scheme which enables mature students to study individual parts of a degree without having to take the whole course.

A few institutions are extremely flexible, allowing freedom for a considerable amount of independent study. Students can decide which skills and knowledge they wish to acquire and how they wish to be assessed at the end of their course. Most colleges and universities accept preparatory courses taken at neighbouring colleges of further education, and, as has been explained, some universities have worked out 'associate' status for local colleges by which earlier parts of a higher education course are 'franchised' to a local college.

A particularly useful source of information is *Higher Education – a Brief Guide for Adults*, published by the Association of Graduate Careers Advisory Services.

Overseas Students

For the purpose of fees and grants, government regulations divide people into home students and overseas students. Home students are eligible for grants from LEAs or central government; overseas students are not. 'Home students' are defined as those who have been ordinarily resident in the UK for three years and not here for the purposes of education during that time. However, family connections with Britain can sometimes work in your favour here, so it is worth contacting the Grant Section of your local LEA for guidance. For full details of UK grants and awards, obtain a copy of a free leaflet, *Student Grants and Loans – a Brief Guide* from your school or college or by writing to the Department for Education. The Association of Commonwealth Universities has a free personal information service and publishes a free booklet, *Taking a First Degree at a University in Britain*.

The newcomers were bemused by the curious antics of the natives.

A major difficulty for non-EC foreign students is fees, since they are much higher than for UK and EC students throughout the whole of British higher education. Students' unions have campaigned vigorously against this policy, but without success. Fees for overseas students vary according to the course. Workshop/lab/practical and vocational courses are more expensive than others. The fees for a degree course can be up to £6,000 a year, and to that should be added £3,000 or more per annum to pay for accommodation, food, clothing, travel, etc.

Applications

Applications from overseas for universities and polytechnics must be made through the UCAS system – see Part 2. Most colleges are part of that system but you should check before applying, as a few colleges offer direct application. Allow plenty of time for correspondence to reach the UK and be replied to by an admissions tutor. Some overseas governments have a procedure for controlling applications to UK universities and colleges; this is sometimes through an embassy or high commission office in Britain, or through the Department for Education or its equivalent in the overseas country. British Council offices overseas carry a lot of information about courses and institutions in the UK, and prospective applicants should first contact their local British Council office.

Documents

In order to gain entry to the UK, overseas students need a number of papers. In the first place, you should carry a letter of acceptance from the department of the university or college, formally offering you a place on a specified course. The course length and starting dates (three years, etc) should be shown on the letter. You will also need your passport and a UK visa.

You should have with you a recommendation from a government department or agency, and a guarantee that someone – the home government, a company or your family – will accept responsibility for the payment of fees and for providing you with sufficient money to live on while you are in the UK.

Agencies

You are advised to apply through a recognised agency if you come from one of the following countries: Brunei, Cyprus, Ghana, Guyana, India, Nigeria, Singapore, Tanzania, Thailand.

The agency in most cases is the British Council (Technical Assistance Training Department), or your country's embassy or high commission in London. All applications for places at UK universities should be made to UCAS through these agencies. Students from other countries should apply direct through UCAS, but are advised to contact the British Council for help and advice.

Entry into Britain

A newcomer who arrives in Britain without all this documentation or proof must be able to satisfy an immigration officer that she or he intends studying in the UK. In this case, the immigration authorities will allow the student into the UK for a short period, in order to allow time for the papers to be prepared and presented to immigration.

Accommodation

Accommodation for overseas students receives very high priority. Efforts will be made to find you a place in residential accommodation within the university or college, at least for your first year. After that you should know how to go about finding a flat or room of your own. All applicants from overseas should read the section on accommodation in the official prospectuses.

English language

It is likely that you will be asked to show proof of your standards of spoken and written English. These have to be good enough for you to be able to follow your course entirely in English. Before being admitted, a university or college may ask to see evidence – certificates or other documents – of your competence in the English language. Many colleges run special preliminary courses in English in September before the main course begins, which will help bring you up to standard.

Before arriving in Britain

Before arriving in Britain you should read *Higher Education in the United Kingdom – a Handbook for Students and their Advisers*, published by Longman.

After arrival

You may have friends or know fellow students already in Britain who can help you. If not, a good place to stay or call at is the International Students' House in London, where you will be welcomed and helped. Most colleges and universities now have a special adviser or a tutor to help overseas students. Accommodation officers will be ready to help you find a place to stay. The strange environment and way of life does present problems for a while. But most overseas students settle very quickly, and cope with the work. The first year is the worst. The newness and differences in working methods have to become familiar, and if a student is struggling with English, problems are likely to arise. However, there are people ready to help. Some places provide classes in English conversation or other forms of special assistance.

Conclusion

This section of the book has run through the gamut of options – far too many to give full weight to them all. You may still think your initial hunch, or the remark of an elder sister or brother or teacher, will remain a deciding factor in your choice of college. It could be that we have simply strengthened a conviction you already held.

Even if you were to apply all the criteria for choosing that we have described, it would be impossible to guarantee that all will be right. It may be that the thing that makes life intolerable will be some unforeseeable condition that neither you nor we can foresee – simply the bad luck to be given a room you detest, a tutor who makes you bristle, running out of money halfway through the year, or inedible hall food.

But if you make your choice by a logical, thoughtful process, and check through the points we have made, and feel satisfied with the ones closest to your heart, you have the best chance of finding the right place. After that you will be ready to make your application – the subject of our next section.

Course choice grid – a way through the jungle

The grid on page 98 shows some criteria we believe may be important: add your own, some of which you may know already and others which emerge as you explore what courses and places have to offer. Do write down what you find out – you will never remember all you need to know. Create your own grid if this is not big enough.

Criteria for choosing

Me: my likes, skills, qualifications, strengths, weaknesses and aspirations
Where can I go with my grades?
Subject: think broadly at first
University or college?
Career in mind: what might cut me off from this?
Sandwich courses
Sponsorship
Professional and vocational courses
A year abroad during the course
Level: diploma or degree (ordinary, honours)

Two, three, four, five or more years?
Course content and nature (eg pure or applied)
Foundation first year
Opportunities to change courses
Course structures and teaching styles; assessment methods
Place: size, location, distance from home
Social: entertainment, male/female ratio, culture, union life, sport, snobbery and values
Special provisions I'd like or need.

Sorting out what to do and where to go

If you have decided that going into higher education is a possibility, the variety of places and courses may look rather frightening. Here is a framework for looking at the issues. With the help of teachers/lecturers, careers staff/officers, parents and friends, as well as guidebooks and particularly prospectuses, you need to sort out how they apply in your situation.

Courses

Entry

- **How do the entrance requirements differ? What is the difference between 'studied' and 'passed'?**
- **Do the prospectuses say anything about the grades required?**
- **What is the attitude to a 'year off'?**

Content

- **Is the course a direct continuation of what I have been studying, or is the content very different?**
- **Do courses with different titles have different content, or courses with different titles have broadly the same content?**
- **Can I start new subjects from scratch?**

Insert institution name along top		Place	Place	Place
Location and living criteria	Example criteria			
	Distance from home			
	Accommodation			
	Style of place			
	Other eg career			
Course criteria	Content			
	Structure			
	Options			
	Grades			

- Do I have to do subsidiary subjects?
- What specialisms/options that might interest me are included?

Structure
- How many subjects can I do to start with, before making a final choice?
- Can I have periods of 'experience' during the course? How long is the course as a result?
- How far can I specialise within the subject?
- Is there a first year/part one common to a number of different courses, eg throughout social sciences, or across a number of engineering courses?

Teaching and examinations
- What seem to be the main ways in which people are taught, or learn – lots of lectures, seminars?
- Do essays, projects and practicals count towards assessment?
- How much 'practical' work is there, eg studio time in art, lab work in science/engineering?
- Do the final exams give exemption from the academic requirements of professional bodies?

Career implications
- By doing this course will I be cutting myself off from career options I might want to leave open? Are there options within the course which would improve my employability, eg computer literacy?

Places
Do remember that you may spend three, four or even more years at an institution: check out the places as well as the courses.

- How far away from home do I want to be?
- Is it distance or time or cost or strangeness that matters?
- Do I want to be in a large city, a small town, on a campus, out in the country?
- What kinds of accommodation are available? What do they cost?
- What kinds of student support facilities are there?
- Are there the social and sports facilities I want?
- Are there facilities for people with my particular disability?

My criteria

- It is important to me that ....

....

....

....

....

....

....

- It is important to me that ....

....

....

....

....

....

....

2. UCAS – Application Procedures

Introduction

In the last few years, major changes have taken place in higher education and they have been paralleled by changes in application procedures.

Up until 1993, applications for places on first degree courses at the 'old' universities went through UCCA – the Universities Central Council on Admissions, and applications to polytechnics and colleges and institutes offering first degree courses went through PCAS – the Polytechnics Central Admissions System. In 1992 and 1993 UCCA and PCAS combined their application forms so that candidates had only one form to contend with. For 1993 entry, they could make five choices for UCCA institutions and four choices for PCAS polytechnics and colleges.

Now the polytechnics have gone – they are the 'new' universities. And many colleges have altered their names. A change was needed on admissions, and so UCAS (the Universities and Colleges Admissions Service) was born.

Making Your Application

> **Applications for university and college first degree courses are made on a single UCAS application form.**

For entry to courses in September–October 1994, applications for full-time and sandwich first degree, DipHE and HND courses at all UK universities (except the Open University), at colleges of higher education, and at colleges of further education are made through UCAS. There are some exceptions to this general rule, for example where degree or HND courses have been validated or approved after the UCAS Handbook was published, but these exclusions are few.

UCAS therefore covers the vast majority of full-time undergraduate study in the UK. The institutions and courses within UCAS are listed in the 1994 UCAS Handbook. For 1994 entry applications, students must apply on the new UCAS application form. The UCAS form can be used to apply to up to eight choices of courses in UCAS. Although there are no restrictions on how you can choose the courses that attract you, the UK Medical Schools and Faculties say that it is in the interests of applicants not to apply for more than five choices of medical or dental courses.

Before Completing the UCAS Form ....

There are jobs to do long before you fill in the UCAS application form.

1. Select a group of universities and colleges that offer the course or courses that you are interested in, and read their prospectuses. If the prospectuses are not in your school or careers library, send a postcard or letter to to the Admissions Officer of the university or college, as in the example, completing it in block capitals.

You ought to say which course interests you, because most of the institutions have different brochures for different faculties, departments and courses.

2. Read each prospectus carefully to make sure:
- **(a) that the institution offers the course you want (don't waste an application by applying for a non-existent course!)**

(b) **that you will be able to satisfy the general requirement for admission at each institution to which you apply**
(c) **that you will be able to satisfy the course requirement for the course you choose at each institution.**

Undergraduate prospectus enquiry

Please send me information about entrance requirements, courses, fees, scholarships, residence, etc.

Name ....
Address ....
....
Proposed course(s) ....
.... Proposed year of entry ....
Signed .... Date ....

If the prospectus does not answer all your questions, write to the institution stating your problem. If you aren't sure whether your A-levels and grades do, or will match the course, ask the admissions officer of the institution concerned. 'Do I have the grades?' in Part 1 has more information on general requirements. Course requirements are listed in the UCAS *University and College Entrance; Official Guide*.

Filling in the UCAS Form

1. **Now that BTEC (and in Scotland, SCOTVEC) qualifications are fully recognised, there is a place on the form to list these results if taken and/or to be taken.**
2. **All applications for undergraduate teacher-training now go on the UCAS form.**

3. An applicant can make eight choices, but you can limit your choice to fewer courses than eight if you wish.

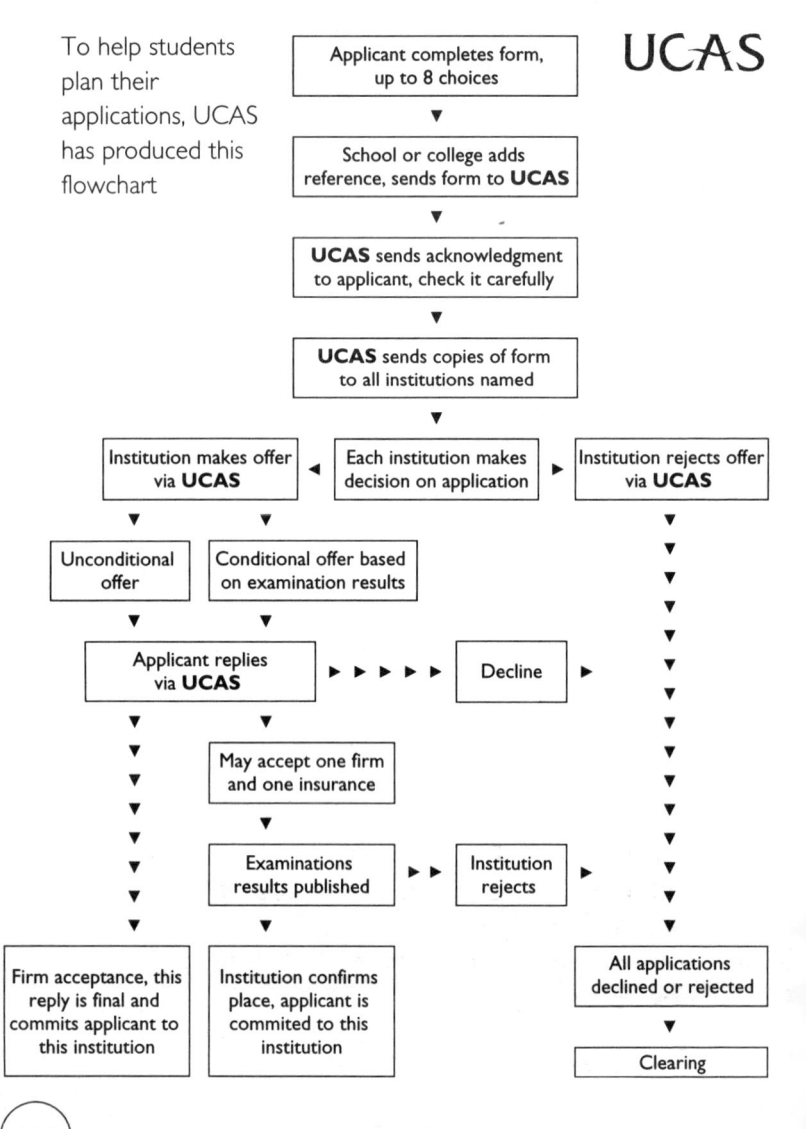

To help students plan their applications, UCAS has produced this flowchart

UCAS

```
Applicant completes form, up to 8 choices
        ▼
School or college adds reference, sends form to UCAS
        ▼
UCAS sends acknowledgment to applicant, check it carefully
        ▼
UCAS sends copies of form to all institutions named
        ▼
Institution makes offer via UCAS  ◄  Each institution makes decision on application  ►  Institution rejects offer via UCAS
        ▼                                                                                      ▼
Unconditional offer   Conditional offer based on examination results
        ▼                    ▼
Applicant replies via UCAS  ► ► ► ► ►  Decline  ►
        ▼       ▼
                May accept one firm and one insurance
                        ▼
                Examinations results published  ► ►  Institution rejects  ►
        ▼               ▼                                                         ▼
Firm acceptance, this reply is final and commits applicant to this institution   Institution confirms place, applicant is commited to this institution   All applications declined or rejected
                                                                                                    ▼
                                                                                                Clearing
```

104

... plainly, with Oliver the ritual of Completing the Form had developed along bizarre lines.

When filling in the form, follow these procedures:
- **Use a black ballpoint pen or black ink.**
- **Check both the institution and course codes carefully and make no errors in entering them.**
- **Make sure that when you enter your interests, they are genuine ones because you may be asked about them at an interview.**
- **Enter information which sets you apart from other candidates (for 'reading', add the names of books you've enjoyed and for 'sport', enter the games you play and the standard to which you play them).**
- **Sign and date the form.**
- **Attach a postal order to cover either or both systems.**

Your headteacher will add the name of your school, write out a reference, check your entry and send it to UCAS some time before the closing date of 15 December. Applicants for Oxford or Cambridge Universities must apply by 15 October. (Early application is an advantage. Don't leave it too near to the closing date.) If you have left school, you will have to ask your former headteacher if he or she would be willing to write a reference for you.

The choices

You should *not* list your entries in order of preference, but in the order in which they appear in the *UCAS Handbook*. Neither should you attempt to place brackets against your choices indicating your preference.

Your choice of institution

This is a very personal decision. As well as consulting the official prospectuses of the institutions, you should also try to get hold of an alternative prospectus or at least the handbook of the students' union. These give an alternative flavour and are usually straightforwardly honest. Your careers adviser can tell you how to do this.

You should also try to talk to someone (a former student of your school, perhaps) who has been to the institution you have provisionally selected, and if you can afford to make a term-time visit to the campus, do so, as it will give you an opportunity to talk to students who are already there.

As the UCAS form requires you to discuss your skills and interests, some tips on how to present yourself may come in handy. You should find that the prompts in Part 1 to assess your skills are relevant here. You can use that information at interviews to help you elaborate your answers and enable you to speak at greater length about yourself.

PART 2 · UCAS

3 APPLICATIONS

(a) Institution code name	(b) Institution code	(c) Course code	(d) Campus code	(e) Course code name	(f) Further requested details	(g) Prev Applic'n (year)	(h) Home	(i) Defer entry
ABRDN	A20	C320		Zool Mar				✓
NOTTM	N84	C300		Zoology				✓
BANGR	B06	C320		Zoo/M Zoo				✓
CAM	C05	Y160		Nat Sci				✓
UCL	U80	C300		Zoology				✓
PLYM	P60	F9FY		Uws/OSc				✓
MANU	M20	C300		Zoology				✓
GLASG	G28	C174		Aquat				✓

Previous applicants through UCCA or PCAS please enter the serial or application number of your most recent application

Example UCAS form

Here is a list of the resources that are important:

- **Your academic record throughout your school career, and particularly in the last three years of school.**
- **Your GCSE or other results – subjects and grades.**
- **The forecast given by the school (and asked of you at interview) of your forthcoming A-level exams.**
- **The coursework you may have gathered together – an art and design folio, or completed projects in craft subjects, for example.**
- **Special skills and evidence of standards reached – in music, for instance.**
- **Your intellectual and academic potential, such as:**
  - **interest in the subject**
  - **ability and intelligence**
  - **willingness to study and work hard**
  - **perseverance and determination.**
- **Your range of interests:**
  - **cultural (theatre, films, books, music, art, etc)**
  - **practical (gardening, cars, electronics, etc)**
  - **reading (what do you read beyond A-level textbooks?)**
  - **sporting (as a player or spectator, games and sports)**
  - **performing (are you involved in music, drama, art, discussions?)**
  - **out of school (clubs, groups, leisure activities).**
- **Work experience:**
  - **any part-time or full-time jobs. If so, what did you do and what did you think about the experience?**
  - **training (have you been on any training schemes or projects?)**
  - **community (have you done any voluntary service or helped the local community?).**

- **Your character and personality: interviewers will be trying to assess your personality in discussion, using their own methods but drawing on the headteacher's report.**
- **Your vocational interests: have you given any thought to a career after qualifying; do you have any half-formed career interests; were these based on your reading, experience, friends or family?**
- **Your contribution: the institution will be looking to see what you can put into the life of the place; will you make a positive contribution or just take from it?**

Your curriculum vitae

Now that you have seen what academic and personal resources are required, you can build up your own dossier. This can be the basis for your UCAS or other application forms. You will need several sheets of paper.

On the first sheet, make a list of all the subjects you have studied at GCSE, A-level or AS. If you have any additional academic accomplishments or awards, list them separately at the end. You could arrange the information like this:

Examinations and grades			
Subject	GCSE grade	A-level grade	AS grade
English language	B		
Maths			C
History	A	Pass at B expected	

Now write out a list or a statement of your interests and activities. You could set it out like this:

At school: clubs, societies, organisations
(a) Sports and games
(b) Clubs
(c) Activities
(d) Other interests
(e) Positions held (treasurer, captain, etc)

In the community and out of school
(a) Sports and games
(b) Clubs
(c) Activities
(d) Other interests

At home
(a) Leisure activities
(b) Reading and other intellectual or creative interests
(c) Practical interests

Work experience or community help
(a) Jobs (list them, with some details)
(b) Any community work
(c) Any training (on a government or company scheme)

Careers
What careers ideas or interests do you have?

Travel and holidays
Have you been anywhere interesting? Are there any places you would particularly like to visit and why?

Miscellaneous
Is there anything else which you think might help your application?

When to Apply

Timing is all-important for applications. Your entry form should normally reach UCAS between 1 September and the following dates:

15 October   Applicants for the universities of Cambridge and Oxford must also submit a separate form or card to the university concerned by this date, in addition to their UCAS applications.

15 December For applicants *not* including Cambridge or Oxford among their entries on the UCAS form.

Late applications (ie those received after 15 December)

It is in your best interests to apply before 15 December. Some applicants, especially those from outside the UK, find this impossible. If you apply late, give your reasons. Late applications will be accepted under the following conditions:

(a) 15 December to end of May

UCAS will forward your application to the institutions

15 October and 15 December were dates seared into Emily's memory.

listed on your form for consideration at their discretion. Decisions on applications received between these dates must be made by institutions by early June.

(b) End of May to 14 August – Clearing
If you apply after May you will be treated as a late applicant and be considered in the Clearing scheme which operates at the end of August and in September. You will be sent a Clearing Entry Form and a clearing instructions leaflet.

Cambridge and Oxford
In addition to your UCAS entry to these universities you *must* make a direct application to them. As they are a special case, refer to the section on them for details.

After You Apply – the UCAS Timetable
After you have sent in the form, the procedure is as follows:
1. **The acknowledgment card is returned to all applicants to indicate that their application forms have been received by UCAS.**
2. **In due course each applicant is sent a computer-printed letter which should be checked carefully as it may disclose an error made on the application form. If there is a mistake in the institution code, the applicant should write to UCAS immediately. A mistake in a course code should be dealt with by writing directly to the institution concerned. The acknowledgment also shows the applicant's personal application number. The time-lag between the issue of the acknowledgment card and the letter increases as the applications season progresses.**
3. **If you are worried about not receiving an acknowledgment, you should first of all get in**

touch with your school to find out when the application form was posted to **UCAS**. If the school is concerned, and a month or more has passed, it should get in touch with **UCAS** for advice.

4. **UCAS** sends reduced-sized copies of the applicant's form simultaneously to each of the institutions chosen on the form. Each institution sees all the other choices that an applicant has made. The institutions consider the applications and inform the applicant, via **UCAS**, of their decision. Some institutions also invite students for interview before deciding. Institutions give a decision by the end of March at the latest for applications reaching them by 15 December.

5. Applicants are asked to reply to any offers when they have received all the decisions from the institutions. You can delay your decision until after attending interviews.

6. From your original eight choices, you can hold one offer as a firm acceptance, and one other offer as insurance.

Conditional Offers

You will either receive a no-strings-attached unconditional offer or an offer that is subject to or conditional upon your attaining certain examination grades in your forthcoming examinations. If you firmly accept the conditional offer, and then reach the standard requested, your chosen institution is obliged to accept you.

If, however, you fail to reach the standard of the conditions, it does not mean that you will be automatically rejected. Institutions often pitch their requests quite high, in the knowledge that not everyone will reach this standard. So any remaining places on the course may be filled by people who are just below the required standard. For a department, this is a very useful method of controlling the number of places. Otherwise, if they announced that, say, three D grade A-levels would be satisfactory, they might have to accept many more people than they have places for.

On the other hand, you should not fall below the grades by more than about one grade. If the institution offers you a place on condition that you reach A-level ABB in three subjects, you stand a good chance if you get BBB, but will probably be unsuccessful with BCC. The competition does depend on supply and demand for places.

It has been explained earlier that when you reply to the offers made to you, you will be able to hold one firm and one insurance offer. The insurance offer will probably have asked for lower grades in your examinations than the firm offer. If you fail to get into your first-choice institution and are rejected, you will be considered for your insurance offer.

Confirmation of Offers

In August, examination results are published. If you have obtained the grades required in the conditions, you will be offered your firm choice. If you are rejected because you don't get the grades, you will be offered your insurance choice, providing you have the necessary A-levels (or ASs). If still rejected, you will go into Clearing.

Clearing

The UCAS Clearing procedures come into effect from mid-August each year and last until late September. Clearing is the final stage of the UCAS scheme. Clearing exists to find vacancies at institutions for applicants with suitable qualifications but whose original applications have been unsuccessful. It is also an alternative for applicants who did not apply at the normal time.

The scramble for places in the Clearing system had taken an ugly turn.

How to apply for Clearing

UCAS automatically send details of the Clearing system:

(a) **in August to applicants who are holding no offers**

(b) **in late August/early September to applicants whose offers are not confirmed.**

Other applicants who did not apply between September and March and who wish to be included in Clearing (eg because their examination results were better than expected) should write to UCAS for the Clearing Application Form and leaflet.

Applying to Cambridge and Oxford

If you wish to apply to these universities *and* others within the UCAS system, refer to the section on applying through these bodies.

In addition to your standard UCAS form with either of these universities and other institutions marked on it, you must make a direct application to Cambridge or Oxford.

> **Remember, you may not apply to Cambridge and Oxford in the same admissions year unless you wish to apply for a choral and/or organ scholarship at both universities.**

Cambridge University

The Cambridge Preliminary Application Form (PAF) must be sent to the admissions tutor of your first-preference Cambridge college or, in the case of an open application, to the Cambridge Intercollegiate Applications Office by 15 October preceding the year of entry (ie 15 October 1994 for an October 1995 entry).

The *Cambridge Admissions Prospectus* gives details of the admissions procedure. Your headteacher should have a copy of this book. You may also obtain it from the Cambridge Intercollegiate Applications Office listed in the Address List.

Conditional offers are made on the basis of PAF, plus school reports and personal interviews. Offers made by the college depend upon public examination grades or performance in Cambridge's own STEP examinations (the Sixth Term Examination Papers) set by the Oxford and Cambridge Schools Examination Board. Anybody may apply to sit the examination, and syllabuses and previous papers can be obtained from the Examination Board.

Oxford University
You must submit an application card to Oxford by 15 October of the year you wish to enter. These are distributed in bulk to schools, together with copies of the university prospectus; you should obtain a copy from your headteacher, or, if you have left school, from the Oxford Admissions Office.

Your application will state which college you wish to join. A successful applicant is accepted by a college or hall, and satisfies the entrance requirements for the university.

Courses Leading to the Basic Professional Social Work Qualification
For courses leading to the Diploma in Social Work (DipSW), awarded by the Central Council for Education and Training in Social Work, you should write to the Council for course details and information on application procedures through the SWAS (Social Work Admissions System).

England, Northern Ireland, Scotland and Wales
Whether you are from England, Northern Ireland, Scotland or Wales, you should be as keen to consider studying in another part of the UK as you are in your own. Qualifications at 18+ differ slightly in both Northern Ireland and Scotland from those in England and Wales. Most institutions, however, set entry requirements in the range of 18+ qualifications: Highers, BTEC national diploma, A-levels, AS and the Scottish Certificate of Sixth Year Studies. And the UCAS system applies to the Scottish universities and the former Central Institutions (now known as centrally funded colleges).

Scotland
You will find differences between studying in Scotland and the

rest of the UK because Scottish colleges have retained their own characteristics. For example, first degree courses are generally of four years' duration and broader than most English and Welsh ones, so that you study combinations of subjects rather than a single subject. To illustrate, arts courses generally include three or four subjects in the first year drawn from a wide range of choices. In subsequent years you study one, two or three subjects, ending up with a degree in, say, Arabic and business studies (Edinburgh) or mathematics and economics (Dundee). Another difference is that almost everyone starts on an 'ordinary' degree course in their first year, moving to the honours course in the second year. *The Entrance Guide to Higher Education in Scotland* (first published in May 1993) is the book which tells you all about the entrance requirements at Scottish universities and colleges.

Centrally funded colleges

These are colleges, much like the former polytechnics, fully recognised as degree-awarding institutions under the 1992 Further and Higher Education Act. They provide a rich variety of courses leading to degrees, higher national diplomas, national diplomas and certificates.

Centrally funded colleges are located in the major Scottish cities and towns. They are all listed in Part 1.

Teaching in Scotland

Scottish secondary school teachers must have a degree or higher diploma and a postgraduate training certificate. Primary teachers need to take a three-year course at a college of education leading to a teaching diploma. For information, consult the *Memorandum on Entry Requirements for Admissions to Courses of Teacher-Training in Scotland.*

Northern Ireland

There are two universities in Northern Ireland: Queen's University of Belfast and the University of Ulster.

Application to the universities is through the UCAS system but application for some courses is direct to the two institutions: check their prospectuses for details of these arrangements.

The Chance of Succeeding

The grade requirements vary a good deal from one institution to another. In general, entry requirements have been getting tougher as the demand for places has grown. Establishments with the greatest prestige naturally insist (though important exceptions are made) on the highest achievement.

In 1992 over half the entrants to Cambridge University had three A-grade A-levels. Over 40 per cent of Oxford entrants had the same, but only 10 per cent of university entrants as a whole had these grades. Scoring lower than BBC or BCC at A-level does not, however, rule out all chances of securing an entry. Depending on subject, pressure of numbers and the standing of the institution, applicants with appreciably lower grades do stand a chance of succeeding. For technological, science and arts courses at the 'new' universities, requirements will vary from A-level grades B to grade E in two or three subjects, along with three or more GCSEs. In some cases, to have studied for a particular A-level will pay some dividends even though you didn't actually *pass* it.

The *Degree Course Guides* are outstanding among the sources of information for degree course requirements. Alternatively, access to the ECCTIS database makes all the relevant facts available (see Part 4).

Competition for a place was intense.

Who applies?

In 1992 over 210,000 'home' applicants (that is, UK and European Community) and 28,000 overseas applicants applied for entry to UK universities through the UCCA system. Of these 238,000 hopefuls, 122,000 applicants gained places at university.

For the polytechnics and colleges, PCAS reported that 241,000 applications were made, of which 103,000 gained admission to first degree, DipHE and HND courses. There is still an overlap between UCCA and PCAS applications but in 1994 this overlap will be ironed out.

Clearly, a lot of applicants do not succeed in gaining a place. However, when looking at the reasons for this failure, it has to be remembered that many are unsuccessful simply because they do not obtain the minimum requirements of two A-level or equivalent passes for entry on to a degree course and one A-level or equivalent pass for an HND course. Many withdraw their applications or are not considered for a place once their public examination results are known.

Suitably qualified applicants

The rule is, then, that if you are able to achieve the necessary grades, forge ahead – your chances are good!

Each September there are vacancies for 'suitably qualified' people. By then examination results have been made public and vacancies become available to suitably qualified late applicants. This generally means 'good' grades in three (but perhaps two) subjects.

Popular subjects

The popularity of subjects varies from year to year. Even so, some subjects retain their popularity and admissions tutors report that the following subjects are consistently popular with applicants:

accountancy/finance	English
architecture	fine art
biochemistry	forestry
biology	geography
business studies	history
computing	law
dentistry	mathematics
design	medicine
drama/theatre studies	pharmacy
economics	veterinary science

In general it is the vocational subjects which are now in vogue. Humanities subjects and social sciences have become less popular. Applications for degree and HND courses in electronics, electronic and electrical engineering and computer science have increased, but so have the number of places available. Universities are keen to offer places on science and technology courses because they get more Government funding for these courses than arts subjects.

Grades that will secure you a place

Popularity makes it *much more* difficult to obtain a college place in some subjects than in others – as long as the increase in applications is outstripping the provision of places.

As admissions tutors are primarily interested in the grades of the applicants, you would expect to find that the most popular courses demand the highest entry grades. And this is indeed the case.

The statistics show that veterinary science and accountancy have for some years been at the head of this 'league table' of difficult subjects to enter. Figures for university entrants show that 90 per cent of people accepted to read veterinary science had *at least* two A-level passes at grade A or B, or three A-level passes at BBB.

The table opposite ranks subjects according to their difficulty in terms of the A-level grades you need to study them. Remember, though, that requirements vary from one institution to another. For the same subject, at one place you could be admitted with, say, three C grades, whereas another will insist on, say, three B grades.

One thing this chart cannot take into account is that where a subject requires non-academic skills, such as education (teacher-training), admissions tutors will be looking for

Subject	Percentage of undergraduates studying the subject with two Bs and an A or better in A-level subjects
veterinary science	90
medicine	64
law	61
accountancy	44
mathematics	42
computer science	36
physics	30
English	30
history	30
aeronautical engineering	28
electrical engineering	28
chemistry	26
French	26
biochemistry	26
architecture	26
mechanical engineering	22
geography	22
music	20
dentistry	20
economics	18
civil engineering	16
psychology	14
geology	14
pharmacy	12
agriculture	12
government and politics	10
education	10
business management	10
biology	9
sociology	6

indicators of aptitude other than exam results. If you feel a vocational inclination towards a subject, you may be lucky enough to find that exam results are not the only requirement asked of you and your other abilities will support your application.

What's in an A-level score?

You will find that entry requirements sometimes talk of the number of points demanded by a course.

A-level and AS scores are calculated on the basis of:
A grade A = 10 points
AS grade A = 5 points
A grade B = 8 points
AS grade B = 4 points
A grade C = 6 points
AS grade C = 3 points
A grade D = 4 points
AS grade D = 2 points
A grade E = 2 points
AS grade E = 1 point
Fail = 0 points

Thus, three ASs with grades AAA = 15 points and two ASs both at grade E = 2 points.

In order to assess likely requirements for various subjects, we asked universities to give their expected A-level offer grades for a range of subjects. From the results, the average scores you would appear to need for various subjects are as shown opposite.

As we noted earlier, requirements vary. For example, in chemistry the grade requirements range from three A-level subjects at AAA to CDD.

Subject	Average A-level points required
veterinary science	26
accountancy and finance	24
medicine	24
law	23
dentistry	21
English medicine	20
forestry	20
pharmacy	20
architecture	19
geology	19
town and country-planning	19
aeronautical engineering	18
biochemistry	18
biology, zoology, botany	18
drama	18
French	18
German	18
history	18
mathematics	18
music	18
agriculture	17
economics	17
geography	17
psychology	17
surveying	17
business and management studies	16
chemistry	16
classical studies and classics	16
computer science	16
electrical engineering	16
government and public administration	16
mechanical engineering	16

philosophy	16
physics	16
zoology	16
sociology	15
theology	15
chemical engineering	14
civil engineering	14

The grades we've listed are approximate. The least that the study of these grades will do is to help you with your UCAS application. It should prevent you from making silly mistakes, such as applying for a course which demands BBB when your own expectation (and that of your teachers) is that you will do well to get CCD in your three A-level subjects.

Something to remember about grades requirements is that many university departments quote low or 'minimum' offers, such as two Cs or even two Es. This is part of their strategy. When offers are made they may well ask for BCC. One of the reasons for this mysterious policy is that the university department does not want to deter good applicants who lack self-confidence: they could drive away good people if they insisted on BCC early in the admissions 'game'. Though it may not be a game for you, there are all the elements of bid and counter-bid in the whole university application–admissions business.

Visits and Open Days

Universities and colleges welcome visits from prospective students. Some of them organise courses and open days for students in the first year of the sixth form. The best publication for precise information on open days is *The Sixth Former's Guide to Visiting Universities, Polytechnics and Colleges*, which is published each January by ISCO. If the place is not too far from your home, pay a visit during term-time; you will only be able to get a true impression of a place while the students are there. You can walk around, get a 'feel' for the place, and talk to students. In general, as long as they are not rushing to a lecture, students will be willing to talk freely.

Before your visit, write to the department you are interested in, and they may invite you to look in or be interviewed at the same time. On your visit, look at lecture rooms, labs and workshops. Ask if it is possible to see the library, student accommodation and sports facilities and, if you can, go into the students' union. While there, look at the noticeboard to see what recreational activities are offered. Making a visit could save you finding out at the interview that you can't stand the place. By then you'll have wasted a space on your application form.

Interviews

Many institutions now offer places without interviewing. This means that admissions staff rely on an application form and the report from your school or referees (which shows how important it is to make full use of them).

You could be interviewed by a single lecturer or by two or three members of staff. Make sure of your travel times and arrive on time. You will have to pay your own fares.

The thought of attending an interview is daunting and worrying for many people. But most admissions tutors are expert at their job and will try to put you at ease. Prepare yourself for the interview by re-reading your application form and rehearsing some of the questions and possible answers, although impromptu answers appeal to interviewers rather than obviously prepared ones. Even so, you should be ready for the obvious questions, however worded, such as:

'What are your reasons for applying for this subject or course?'
'Why have you chosen this university or college?'
'What do you hope to do after graduating?'
'How did you find out about us?'

Robert was quite unprepared for such a gruelling interview.

Be ready, too, for this question: 'Do you want to ask us anything?' Remember that you are also interviewing them. This is your chance to assess the course, the department and the university.

The form of an interview varies a great deal. If there are a large number of people applying to a department where few places will be offered, you have done well to get an interview. With plenty to choose from, the interview is likely to be testing and fairly lengthy. On the other hand, where there are few applicants, the interviewer will be trying to 'sell' the course to you. This is particularly true of science and engineering courses where departments try to recruit their fair share of able applicants, and you may be one of them. So they will try hard to impress you.

For any interview, of course, you should be clean and tidy – and punctual! Admissions tutors and lecturers are generally impressed by people who can talk freely and on a range of topics. They are looking for knowledge of the subjects being studied, an alert mind and some self-confidence. But don't be long-winded or too cocky. Just be natural and and do not be afraid to say that you do not know the answer to a specific question.

If you are at school, your tutor or one of your teachers will probably organise a practice interview if you ask. If this is not possible, ask a friend to put you through your paces. There are many books on interviews and interview technique; many of these will be in your local library.

Presenting yourself effectively

Every piece of information that an interviewer gathers about you, everything you say – or do – builds up an impression! The impression you want to put over is that you are the right person for the college place (and later, for a job).

The impression you give to an interviewer is conveyed by these things:
- **what you look like – your appearance, so be smart**
- **what you say in answer to questions – so be prepared for questions about yourself, your school career, your likes and dislikes**
- **how you structure your answers – 'yes' or 'no' aren't very helpful, so be prepared to give short, to-the-point answers**

- **the way you talk – accents are perfectly OK but ungrammatical and indistinct answers won't impress**
- **body language and facial expressions – try to appear attentive but relaxed, waving arms (or legs) isn't impressive**
- **your reaction – how you react to what an interviewer says and does (tears or tantrums should be avoided!)**
- **your general attitude and manner – the best advice is to be controlled and polite, and not effusive, too talkative or too laid-back**
- **the questions you ask – so have one or two already thought out**
- **your performance on written or practical tests and exercises.**

To summarise: you have to put over a positive attitude – be keen, alert, willing to listen and respond intelligently, and all those positive aspects can be practised and improved.

For help, read *Excel at Interviews* by Patricia McBride published by Hobsons.

Interview experience
Jess Blandford

My very first interview was terrible. I was not at all prepared for the grilling I received. I had gone to the interview with a fixed expectation and was completely thrown by the fact that the interviewer wanted to talk about different things, and I was, not surprisingly, rejected. The next interview I had was very different. We talked a lot about the books and authors I had quoted on my UCCA form (I applied for English) and it was very relaxed. It involved, as did a couple, being shown a poem and being asked to talk about it.

All the places that asked to interview me wanted to see some of my A-level work. In most cases the essays formed the basis of the interview, which meant I was at least partially prepared. Newcastle sent a questionnaire containing five long-answer questions instead of an interview.

The biggest mistake I made in my interviews was to have prepared answers, which meant that I panicked at a question I had not anticipated. What I think they really want is to see you think, rather than test you on what you already know. If possible I think it is good preparation to have a mock interview with a member of staff at your college or school to get a sense of what you can expect.

The subject that you want to study also has a huge effect on the type of interview you can expect. Friends of mine who applied to read science degrees had interviews that seemed more like the interviewer trying to sell the place to the student than a test of the applicant. Whereas interviews for arts degrees, because there is more competition for places, are perhaps more challenging.

Although it is much easier to say than to do, the most important things to remember are to try to relax, and to show your enthusiasm for the subject.

3. Accommodation, Money, the Gap Year

Once you receive a confirmed offer you can sit back and celebrate – you've made it. Nearer the time there will be new concerns: Where am I going to live? Will I have enough money? Will I cope with the work? This section deals with answers to questions like these.

Typical Accommodation

Knowing what to expect in the way of 'digs' in your first year will keep you – and your parents – happy. The following are the most common options.

Traditional halls of residence

These have mostly single rooms arranged in blocks or on corridors, sometimes men only or women only, sometimes mixed. In a study-bedroom you could expect to find a bed, desk, reading lamp, two chairs, bookshelves and a wardrobe. Rooms might – or might not – have a washbasin. Furniture is sometimes moveable so students can rearrange it; at other places you will find beds and wardrobes are fixtures. Meals are provided in the refectory or dining hall, probably self-service, for breakfast, lunch and evening meal.

Self-catering flats and houses

To cut staffing costs, some institutions provide flats. The study-bedrooms are generally grouped in corridors or blocks, and between four to eight rooms share a kitchen and possibly a communal dining area. Electric kettles, cookers, fridges and ironing facilities are normally provided in halls or flats, but not always, so you should check. Residents usually have to bring their own cooking utensils, crockery and cutlery. Blocks of flats like these often have television rooms and lounges.

The accommodation was a novel experience.

Private accommodation

This expression covers the private arrangements which students enter into: renting, leasing, and so on. First-year students are warned against looking for their own accommodation until they have settled into their studies (ie in their second year). Students' unions usually have a welfare service, offering advice on rents, leases, difficulties with landlords, and so on.

Approved lodgings

Many institutions just cannot place all their first-year students in halls of residences or flats. Their accommodation or welfare officers keep lists of approved lodgings. These are private residences with a history of taking in students. They may provide just a room, bed and breakfast, or an evening meal too. There are two kinds of financial arrangement: students pay monthly (usually in advance) direct to the landlord, or to the college, which reimburses the landlord.

At home

Where students live within, say, ten miles of the university or college they enter, most institutions insist that they should live at home. Indeed, some students prefer to be at home, feeling that with a comfortable, familiar environment, and all worries about cooking and cleaning removed, they can concentrate better on academic work.

Allocation of Places ································

Universities and colleges do not have a common policy on placing students. However, they generally try to follow these lines:

1. First-year students

Each student is sent an application form for accommodation, with a request to state preferences – hall, self-catering flat, single sex or mixed accommodation, etc. The selection is then made by the accommodation officer and wardens. All try their best to place first-year students in halls or flats near to the teaching areas – some achieve 100 per cent success, others have to be satisfied with 60 to 70 per cent. The remainder are accommodated in approved lodgings.

2. Students in subsequent years

For a place in a hall of residence or a flat in your following year, you normally have to apply in the spring term of your current year. Some universities and colleges can find places for up to 40 to 50 per cent of applicants. Thereafter, you must ask the accommodation officer for a list of approved lodgings and consider renting privately. By this time, you will have found a group a friends and living out can be far more free and easy. It

does test friendships though, as well as teach you to budget, shop sensibly and to share household tasks. It sounds trivial, but a fridge of mouldy food or a blocked toilet, which no one will arrange to get fixed, will soon create tension among the best of friends.

It isn't possible to list every kind of thing to look for when viewing accommodation, but these points are really important!

- *Financial arrangements* – **weekly, monthly, three-monthly, termly, in advance, through a third person (the college, a letting agency, etc). Ask if there is a rent book (required by law).**
- *Letting agreement* – **is there a letting contract/lease or letting agreement to avoid being evicted at short notice?**
- *Sharing* – **do you have your own room, or is it shared? Are the kitchen, toilet, bathroom shared, and with whom? What financial arrangements affect sharing?**
- *Services* – **who pays for electricity, gas, water? Again, is there a written agreement on this as part of the contract or lease?**
- *Is it a slum?* – **look for evidence of damp, leaks. What heating is provided and how is it paid for?**
- *Key money* – **some landlords ask for 'key money', a payment when the key is handed over rather like a purchase. Ask if there is one, and if it's part of the lease/contract. If not, why not? Is it an extra, then?**
- *Household equipment* – **is the flat or house furnished or unfurnished?. If furnished, what is provided – fridge, kitchen equipment, cooker, bed, lamps, bulbs, and wardrobe, etc? Ask to see and sign an inventory.**
- *What do you have to provide?* – **bed linen, obviously. But what else has to be provided – kitchen utensils, curtains, etc?**

The list could go further, so be sure to call on the students' union or the college welfare office for advice.

3. Postgraduate students
Only full-time, registered postgraduate students are normally eligible for accommodation, and priority is given to applicants in their first year.

4. Disabled students
Some universities and colleges maintain special accommodation for disabled students. Write to the registrar for details (see Part 1).

5. Mature students
In addition, some places have a few reserved flats for married students. Others try to place mature students in postgraduate halls or flats. Again, look through the prospectus or ask for details (see Part 1).

6. Overseas students
High priority is given to placing overseas students in university or college accommodation. A senior member of staff is usually delegated to advise overseas students on rents, places to stay, and other factors about living in Britain (see Part 1).

Fees and Charges

The university or college will have a fixed scale of charges, and students are expected to pay within two weeks of the beginning of term. This can be a problem for students awaiting grants. The average weekly charge varies a great deal, and can be anywhere between £40 and £60 a week. The charges usually distinguish between rent and charges for food. Notice in writing of about four weeks is normally needed if a student wishes to withdraw permanently from residence at the end of term. Except in unusual circumstances, no rebates are given for students who withdraw from hall before the end of term.

Vacations

Postgraduates, final-year and overseas students may apply to stay in residence for vacations, although since most colleges rent out accommodation for conferences it is wise to check up on availability during vacations.

Problems in Finding Accommodation

In your first year, you shouldn't have any problems unless you accept an offer just before term begins, when accommodation has already been allocated. However, do take this advice from an accommodation officer:

The difficulties you may meet in finding a suitable place to live depend to a large extent on the area in which your college is situated and the college itself. Ask your course tutor at the interview who the accommodation or welfare officer is and how to get in touch with him or her. You should write or, better still, telephone the officer, well in advance of your arrival at college. Many colleges have halls of residence, but more often than not they cannot possibly offer rooms to all their students. The earlier you apply, therefore, the better. The race for accommodation doesn't only apply to the halls. Because of the sizes of the halls, many colleges operate a system whereby places are offered to first and final-year students only, and those in their second year must move out of their rooms into other accommodation. This obviously increases the competition for accommodation outside the halls.

Small Towns

If you are intending to study in a relatively small city or town, and if your university or college is not large, then you may find accommodation fairly easily. In these circumstances, the type of accommodation offered may be bed and breakfast in a house with a long-standing connection with the college.

This form of accommodation can present difficulties. There may be fixed meal-times, set times to pay the rent, and possibly a lack of privacy. You should check whether the accommodation is offered through the vacation, and whether or not you have to pay during that period. Your protection under the law is not quite so complete in any accommodation where there is a resident landlord or landlady.

Big City Life!

Finally, on accommodation, here is some advice from a students' union representative.

In a large city the competition is tough. You will find yourself in competition not only with other students but also with homeless families, single people from areas of high unemployment, and others desperate to move out of sub-standard accommodation. For this reason always inspect your room(s) before signing an agreement. Look, too, for damp, leaks, the type of heating, and how it is paid for, ie meter or otherwise (it may be included in your rent). Try to think about how the place will stand up to very wet winters. Ask for a rent book and get it signed as proof of payment. Check the inventory in the presence of the landlord/lady and make sure that the present condition of the items is noted. Get a copy of the tenancy agreement. In short, go over everything. An initial payment of cash will be needed, so be prepared to pay a week's or a month's rent in advance.

Every city has a number of accommodation agencies, but this will involve more money, so don't use them if you can help it. If you have to, go to the long-established ones. Remember you have no legal obligation to pay for the supply of names and addresses, only for an actual service such as an inspection of the property. Some agencies are free: see your students' union or accommodation officer for a list. Local papers are useful sources, but you do have to be quick.

A lot of success in finding good, cheap accommodation comes through who, rather than what, you know. Get to know the final-year students on your course and around your college or university. They may be able to pass their accommodation on to you when they leave. If you think the rent is too high in comparison with others in your area, you may be able to have it reduced by the rent officer or, in the case of an unprotected tenant, the rent tribunal.

Paying Your Way

To be a student is to be hard up. Students are notorious for their lack of cash. We deal briefly with the financial aspects of student life here. For much more information on all sources of funds and all sorts of ideas for jobs, read *Hard Cash!*, published by Hobsons.

There are various sources of money. These are the main ones.

Mandatory awards

If you are 18 or over, and you've been offered a place on an advanced or higher education course, you should qualify for what's called a mandatory award. You will have to check that your course is designated by the Department for Education or the Scottish Office Education Department and that you are eligible. Contact your local education authority or the SOED for up-to-date information.

The award pays your tuition fees and the sum you collect at the beginning of term. This part of the award is for food, rent, travel, etc and is means-tested; your parents must declare their incomes, and their wealth determines your 'grant'. Under present rules, students get no help if their parents' residual income (after tax and National Insurance) is more than £31,000 a year. Those students whose parents' joint residual income exceeds £13,630 will find their grants reduced. Only 25 per cent of students receive the full grant and 20 per cent get no grant at all.

So a student whose parents are retired, unemployed or who earn very little, is likely to get the full award, whereas a student whose mum or dad is a high earner may get nothing. And there is a scale in between. The general idea is that your parents will make up the difference between what you get and the maximum award, although, unfortunately, this does not always happen.

The best guides to grants are the DFE *Grants to Students - a Brief Guide* and its SOED equivalent *Guide to Student Allowances*.

Student loans

In September 1990 the government introduced a Student Loans Scheme as a top-up to the standard grant, and more and more students are now relying on loans to get them through. The loans are designed to be additions to your existing sources of finance – your award, your vacation work, your savings. This is because you do have to pay the loan back from the April after you finish your course and you do have to pay interest at the prevailing rate of inflation. Student loans are administered by the government agency, the Student Loans Company Ltd, based in Glasgow. Students can apply for a loan at any time during the academic year. For example, you may be able to manage for two terms, and then need a loan for the summer term.

PART 3 · ACCOMMODATION, MONEY, THE GAP YEAR

Gerald's mother was horrified, his father stoic, as Gerald remained unable to deal intelligently with his debts.

Discretionary awards

This phrase means that an award is made 'at the discretion' of a local education authority which decides whether to give the grant according to the LEA's own rules.

These awards are getting fewer and fewer. In the past, some LEAs gave generous discretionary awards to students aged 16 to 18 on college courses, or to postgraduate students, or to students who were in particular financial difficulties, perhaps caused by a handicap or by family problems.

The LEAs ration these awards very strictly and you'll be lucky to get one. To apply, you need to get a college place and then apply by letter to the LEA, giving your personal and financial background.

Sponsorship

Sponsorship of a student by a commercial company or the Armed Forces gives the student direct financial help. There are three kinds of sponsorship:

1. **A student is paid an annual salary during all or part of his or her course.**
2. **A student receives a wage or salary while working for an employer during the industrial training part of a sandwich course or while working during vacations.**
3. **A student works for a sponsor for a full year before going to university or college, and is paid both for this year and for any other periods of training during or after the course.**

In return the student may agree to work for the sponsor after graduating. This used to be seen as an unwelcome tie, but with jobs so scarce it is now regarded as a real bonus. (See Part I for more about sponsorship.)

There are various publications on sponsorship; probably the best is *The Which? Guide to Sponsorship in Higher Education*.

Working your way through college

Most students add to their funds by taking on part-time or vacation jobs. These can be anything from carting heavy postbags to washing up. There are several books which can help you find these jobs. Among them are *Summer Jobs in Britain* and *Hard Cash!* If you want to combine work with travel through your vacations, see *Summer Jobs Abroad* and contact BUNAC.

If all else fails, you can borrow, but this must be by far the *worst* option, because you will be paying a high interest rate and volunteering to carry your debts for who knows how many years. A stint doing summer jobs in Britain, Europe or around the world sounds like much more fun!

The Council Tax

In April 1993, the Council Tax replaced the Community Charge. The amount of tax a person pays is determined by the value of the property he or she owns or lives in. Student halls of residence, hostels or other properties where only students live are exempt from the Council Tax. Students living with their parents or other non-students are eligible for the personal discount of 25 per cent.

A Year Off

A year out before higher education is now a common experience. If used constructively there are a lot of **advantages** and it could be an opportunity you'll never have again to do something unusual.

- **You could use the time to gain work experience in a field of specific interest, or general experience of a working environment.**
- **Employers much prefer applicants who have previous experience to offer.**
- **It may enable you to return to the company for vacation work.**
- **By taking a year off and doing something different for that time, you will mature and gain new experiences, and it will be to your advantage if you bring these to your studies.**

There are various options. Among them are these:
- **To take a special one-year course in, say, a foreign language, with a period of residence in the foreign country.**

- **To join a student or youth project for a year and work in the community or at a camp.**
- **To take a foundation or bridging course as preparation for an HE course, or to take a one-year course which is completely different from a proposed college course.**
- **To have a complete break from academic studies – maybe travel the world on a shoestring.**

Faced with her bank statement, Juliet resigned herself to the indefinite postponement of her Himalayan trekking plans.

On the other hand, there are **disadvantages**:
- **During a recession, it is not easy to get a job for a full year, particularly one that is directly relevant to your course. The last thing you want to do is waste months making job applications.**
- **You will also be competing with 18 year-olds looking for permanent jobs.**
- **Some science and maths departments prefer students who come straight from school.**

- **After a year away from studying, you may find it difficult to revive the discipline you'll need and to re-engage your interest.**

Fit for Adventure

If a year off before a higher education course seems a good idea to you, write to the appropriate university or college department and tell them what you intend to do. Most will approve of your action and will tell you to apply for entry for the following year.

There are hundreds of ways to spend a year off. A few are listed above. If you are interested in the idea, there are lots of books which list organisations who will be able to help you. Start with *A Year Off . . . A Year On?* from Hobsons and *A Year Between* published by the Central Bureau for Educational Visits and Exchanges.

4. Where to Find Out More

Experts, books, computers – all these sources will be able to give you information about courses and qualifications. So there's no excuse for not knowing – the information is all there, waiting for you.

First, the **experts**. Your school or college should have a year tutor, careers teacher or a subject teacher who knows about the procedures for applying to university or college. If not, get in touch with your local careers office. They can also tell you about the links between particular courses and careers and help you decide your next move.

Next, **books**. One way of finding out which courses or subjects are directly linked to, or required, for a particular career is to read *Which Subject? Which Career?* (see the 'Book List'). This book tells you about careers from A to Z and lists the courses that are good preparation for those careers.

If you know which subject you want to study but don't know where, or you want to compare different courses on one subject around the country, then the *Degree Course Guides* are essential reading. An expert in each field lists the institutions offering the subject, describes the content of the courses, gives you a flavour of what it's like at each place, tells you the entry requirements and points to likely career paths. Subject by subject the series covers 35 areas of study. You can buy the one for the subject you're interested in, or look for the bound volume in your careers library. They are all published by Hobsons. There's more information in the 'Book List'.

If you just want to browse through lists of courses for ideas about what you might study, there are several books which can help, such as the UCAS *University and College Entrance; Official Guide*.

For university and college entry regulations, you must consult the *UCAS Handbook* and *A Registration Scheme for Application to Art and Design Courses*, which is the ADAR handbook for entry to BTEC higher national and first degree art and design, media and communication courses.

These books list institutions alphabetically and provide some details of every course that each institution has on offer.

There are other books which you can consult: for example there's one for Scottish colleges called *The Entrance Guide for Higher Education in Scotland*.

To find out about one particular institution, write to the institution's admissions office asking for their free prospectus.

Third, **computers**. ECCTIS 2000 is an information service on computer which is provided by the Department for Education. It is managed by a consortium comprising British Telecom, the Careers Research and Advisory Council (CRAC), Hobsons Publishing PLC, UCAS and The Times Network System (TTNS). It is always being updated and carries information on approximately:

- **66,000 courses in higher education**
- **250 professional bodies**
- **numerous qualifications.**

The professional bodies have supplied ECCTIS with details of their entry examinations, and the varied and substantial employer information includes their areas of interest, graduate opportunities, career paths and so on. This database is the backbone of such directories as *GET* (Graduate Employment and Training) and *HIT* (Handbook of Information Technology).

You can search for HE courses information by:
- **subject**
- **type of course**
- **method of study**
- **institution type**
- **location**
- **institution name**
- **UCAS course code**
- **ECCTIS reference number.**

ECCTIS will then display details of courses which match your requirements listing the course title, duration, mode of study (eg, full-time or part-time), qualification awarded, entry requirements, the address and telephone number of the college or university, and information about the course structure and content. CATS information is also given where this has been provided by the institution.

As the system is computerised it can bring together all sorts of information to answer your queries; information that you would have to spend ages looking for in books. New student information services are being added all the time.

ECCTIS can be particularly useful during the Clearing process since it holds up-to-date vacancy information. ECCTIS also supports TV and radio help-line services during Clearing.

You should be able to find ECCTIS in your school or college, the local library or your careers office. But if you have no luck, contact ECCTIS 2000 direct (see the 'Address List').

Address List

These are the addresses of organisations referred to in the text.

Association of Graduate Careers Services (AGCAS)
Central Services Unit, Crawford House, Precinct Centre,
Manchester M13 9EP

Business and Technology Education Council (BTEC)
Information Services, Central House, Upper Woburn Place,
London WC1H 0HH Tel: 071-413 8400

BUNAC (Student Work Abroad)
16 Bowling Green Lane, London EC1R 0BD Tel: 071-251 3472

Cambridge Intercollegiate Applications Office
Kellet Lodge, Tennis Court Road, Cambridge CB2 1QJ

Central Council for Education and Training in Social Work
Derbyshire House, St Chad's Street, London WC1H 8AD

City and Guilds of London Institute
76 Portland Place, London W1N 4AA Tel: 071-278 2468

COMETT is the European Community Action Programme for
Education and Training for Technology.
Commission of the European Communities
200 rue de la Loi, 1049 Brussels, Belgium

ECCTIS 2000 Ltd
Fulton House, Jessop Avenue, Cheltenham, Gloucestershire
GL50 3SH Tel: 0242 518724

International Students' House
229 Great Portland Street, London W1N 5HD

International Students' Housing Society Ltd
International House, 109 Brook Hill Road, Woolwich,
London SE18 6RZ

LINGUA European Communities Commission
8 Storey's Gate, London SWIP 3AT

Oxford and Cambridge Schools Examination Board
PO Box 241, Cambridge CB1 2QR

Oxford Colleges Admissions Office
University Offices, Wellington Square, Oxford OX1 2JD

Scottish Education Department
Gyleview House, 3 Redheughs Rigg, South Gyle
Edinburgh EH12 9HH

SKILL, 336 Brixton Road, London SW9 7AA. SKILL provides
information and advice on facilities in higher education.

Student Loans Company Ltd
100 Bothwell Street, Glasgow G2 7JD Tel: 0345 800500

Universities and Colleges Central Council for Admissions
System (UCAS)
Fulton House, Jessop Avenue, Cheltenham, Gloucestershire
GL50 3SH

Book List

The 'Book List' includes all books referred to in the text and
others, but it is not exhaustive. Most of them are in schools or
local libraries and careers offices. Publishers' names and
addresses are given should you want to buy any of them, but
make sure you ask the current price – some are expensive.

Degree Course Guides

Hobsons Publishing PLC, Bateman Street, Cambridge CB2 1LZ

This series of 35 booklets is written by lecturers in the various subjects. They are the only publications to provide objective information comparing course content. Half the series is revised and published each year, so that each guide is updated every two years. They are available individually and as two bound volumes.

How to use the guides

Suppose you have decided on a foreign language. You could look at the guides for French, German, Italian or Russian. Then let's assume you choose German. There are over 80 institutions offering degree-level courses in German. They are all listed in the *German Degree Course Guide*. So you can find out where the courses are offered and then narrow down the choice to five or six places for your application form.

Content

The guides tell you about the content of the courses, how the subject is taught, how your work is assessed, the examinations, dissertations, and so on. If there are substantial differences between courses with similar names, these are explained, and in many cases the variations are tabulated for easy reading. The guides also tell you about entrance requirements, selection procedures, application methods and timings, and selection interviews.

Jobs

Each guide has a special section called 'Graduate Outlook'. This tells you about opportunities for employment. This section is written by an expert – such as a graduate careers service adviser.

The Guides

The *Degree Course Guide* series covers the following areas of study:

Agricultural sciences
Architecture, landscape architecture and planning
Art and design studies
Biochemistry
Biological sciences (including biology, botany, cell and marine biology, genetics and zoology)
Business, management and accountancy
Chemistry
Classics
Computer science
Dentistry
Economics
Engineering technology (including engineering and engineering science; chemical engineering; civil engineering including building; electrical and electronic engineering; materials engineering, materials science and metallurgy; mechanical and manufacturing engineering; mining engineering and mineral processing; surveying)
English (including American studies, Celtic studies and drama)
Food Science and Technology with Hotels, Catering and Tourism
French
Geography
Geological and environmental sciences
German (including Dutch and Scandinavian studies)
History (including archaeology)
Italian and Hispanic studies
Law
Mathematics and statistics
Medicine

Microbiology and immunology
Music
Pharmacy and pharmacology (including related medical studies)
Philosophy
Physics
Physiology (including anatomy and human biology)
Politics (including international relations)
Psychology
Russian and Oriental studies (including African studies)
Social sciences (including sociology, social administration and anthropology)
Theology and religious studies
Veterinary science

A Registration Scheme for Application to Art and Design Courses
ADAR, Penn House, 9 Broad Street, Hereford HR4 9AP

A Year Between
Central Bureau for Educational Visits and Exchanges, Seymour Mews, London W1H 9PE

A Year Off . . . A Year On? 1992 edition
Hobsons Publishing PLC, Bateman Street, Cambridge CB2 1LZ

Cambridge Admissions Prospectus
CIAO, Kellet Lodge, Tennis Court Road, Cambridge CB2 1QJ

Cambridge University Handbook
Cambridge University Press, Edinburgh Building, Shaftesbury Road, Cambridge CB2 2RU

Courses Directory
Published by ECCTIS, this lists Access courses throughout the country.

Degree Course Offers
An annual guide to higher education admission. It gives the average entry grades for each degree course. Trotman and Co Ltd, 12 Hill Rise, Richmond, Surrey TW20 6UA

Directory of Further Education 1993/4
A complete guide to all further education, professional and vocational courses in the UK. Hobsons Publishing PLC, Bateman Street, Cambridge CB2 1LZ

Directory of Higher Education 1993/4
An annual publication describing over 15,000 first degree, HNC/D, DipHE and professional courses in the UK. Hobsons Publishing PLC, Bateman Street, Cambridge CB2 1LZ

Entrance Guide to Higher Education in Scotland
COSHEP, St Andrew House, 141 West Nile Street, Glasgow G1 2RN

Excel at Interviews
Hobsons Publishing PLC, Bateman Street, Cambridge CB2 1LZ

First Destinations of University and Polytechnic Graduates
AGCAS Central Services Unit, Crawford House, Precinct Centre, Oxford Road, Manchester M13 9EP

GET 94, Graduate Employment and Training
Hobsons Publishing PLC, Bateman Street, Cambridge CB2 1LZ
The most comprehensive graduate careers directory. It includes full profiles of over 400 employers of graduates and an A–Z directory listing over 3,000. It covers over 70,000 jobs and courses open to graduates.

Grants to Students – a Brief Guide
Department for Education, Publications Centre, Government Buildings, Honeypot Lane, Stanmore, Middlesex HA7 1AZ

The Students' Guide to Higher Education
An annual guide which lists colleges and institutions of higher education and describes their courses. Standing Conference of Principals, Edge Hill College of Higher Education, St Helens Road, Ormskirk, Lancashire L39 4QP

Guide to Students' Allowances
Scottish Office Education Department, Awards Branch, Gyleview House, 3 Redheughs Rigg, South Gyle, Edinburgh EH12 9HH

The NATFHE Handbook of Initial Teacher-Training
Linneys ESL, Newgate Lane, Mansfield, Nottinghamshire NG18 2PA

Hard Cash! Paying your way through college: working opportunities and sources of funds
Hobsons Publishing PLC, Bateman Street, Cambridge CB2 1LZ

Higher Education – a Brief Guide for Adults
AGCAS Gives advice for mature students *(see pages 90-91)*

Higher Education in the United Kingdom – a Handbook for Students and their Advisers
Longman Group Ltd, Longman House, Burnt Mill, Harlow, Essex CM20 2JE
Also obtainable from the Association of Commonwealth Universities and the British Council. Useful for overseas students.

HIT 94 The Handbook of Information Technology
Hobsons Publishing PLC, Bateman Street, Cambridge CB2 1LZ
A comprehensive guide to the work available in information technology.

How to Apply for Admission to a University
UCAS, Fulton House, Jessop Avenue, Cheltenham,
Gloucestershire GL50 3SH
An annual publication.

Mature Students – University Degree Courses
The Committee of Vice-Chancellors and Principals,
29 Tavistock Square, London WC1 9EZ

Memorandum on Entry Requirements for Admissions to Courses of Teacher-Training in Scotland
TEACH, PO Box 165, Edinburgh EH8 8AI

The Potter Guide to Higher Education
Dalebank Books, 4–8 Bank Lane, Denby Dale, Huddersfield,
West Yorkshire HD8 8QP
An annual and independent guide to student life at UK institutions.

The 1994 Sixth Former's Guide to Visiting Universities, Polytechnics and Colleges
The ISCO Careers Information Service, 12a–18a Princess Way,
Camberley, Surrey GU15 3SP

Sponsorships
Published by COIC.
Available from Department CW ISCO 5, The Paddock, Frizinghall,
Bradford BD9 4HD
Lists sponsorships that are available.

Student Grants and Loans – a Brief Guide
Department for Education, Publications Centre, Government Buildings, Honeypot Lane, Stanmore, Middlesex HA7 1AZ

The Students' Guide to Educational Credit Transfer
ECCTIS, Fulton House, Jessop Avenue, Cheltenham, Gloucestershire GL50 3SH

Students and Sponsorship 1994
Hobsons Publishing PLC, Europa House, St Matthew Street, London SW1P 2JT
A magazine giving advice and general information about sponsorship.

Summer Jobs Abroad and *Summer Jobs in Britain*
Vacation Work Ltd, 9 Park End Street, Oxford OX1 1HJ

Taking a First Degree at a University in Britain
The Association of Commonwealth Universities, John Foster House, 36 Gordon Square, London WC1H 0PF
A free booklet giving advice for overseas students studying in Britain.

The Which? Guide to Sponsorship in Higher Education
Consumers' Association, 2 Marylebone Road, London NW1 4DX
A guide to companies and institutions with sponsorship arrangements.

UCAS Handbook
UCAS, Fulton House, Jessop Avenue, Cheltenham, Gloucestershire GL50 3SH

University and College Entrance; Official Guide
Sheed and Ward, 14 Cooper's Row, London EC3N 2BH
An annual guide to university and college entrance.

Volunteer Work
Central Bureau for Educational Visits and Exchanges,
Seymour Mews, London W1H 9PE

What Do Graduates Do?
Hobsons Publishing PLC, Bateman Street, Cambridge CB2 1LZ
An annual record of the destinations of first-year graduates.

Which Degree?
Hobsons Publishing PLC, Bateman Street, Cambridge CB2 1LZ
A comprehensive and extensive guide for students applying for a degree course. Published in five volumes, each covering a range of subjects.

Which Subject? Which Career?
Consumers' Association and Hobsons Publishing PLC. Available from Hobsons.
A guide to the links between degree and HND subjects and possible careers.

Working Holidays 1994
Central Bureau for Educational Visits and Exchanges, Seymour Mews, London W1H 9PE

The Higher Education Institutions: Names, Addresses, Telephone Numbers

As this publication goes to press, a few institutions are awaiting approval of their new names. Readers are asked to check directly with the institution and, if possible, via the UK Courses Information Service, ECCTIS, found in many libraries and careers offices.

We have divided this list of institutions into four categories:
I – 'Old' Universities in the UK
  – England
  – Northern Ireland
  – Scotland
  – Wales
II – 'New' Universities
III – Scottish Centrally Funded Colleges
IV – Colleges and Institutes of Higher Education

I 'Old' Universities in the UK
England
Aston University, Aston Triangle, Birmingham B4 7ET
021-359 6313

University of Bath, Claverton Down, Bath BA2 7AY
0225 826826

University of Birmingham, Edgbaston, Birmingham B15 2TT
021-414 3344

University of Bradford, Richmond Road, Bradford BD7 1DP
0274 733466

University of Bristol, Senate House, Tynedale Avenue, Bristol
BS8 1TH 0272 303030

Brunel University, Kingston Lane, Uxbridge, Middlesex UB8 3PH
0895 274000

University of Buckingham, Hunter Street, Buckingham
MK18 1EG 0280 814080

University of Cambridge, Intercollegiate Applications Office, Kellet Lodge, Tennis Court Road, Cambridge CB2 1QJ
0223 333308

City University, Northampton Square, London EC1V 0HB
071-477 8000

Cranfield Institute of Technology at the Royal Military College of Science, Shrivenham, Swindon SN6 8LA 0793 785400

University of Durham, Old Shire Hall, Durham DH1 3HP
091 374 2000

University of East Anglia, Norwich NR4 7TJ 0603 56161

University of Essex, Wivenhoe Park, Colchester CO4 3SQ
0206 873666

University of Exeter, Northcote House, The Queen's Drive, Exeter EX4 4QJ 0392 263263

University of Hull, Cottingham Road, Hull, North Humberside HU6 7RX 0482 46311

Keele University, Keele, Newcastle-under-Lyme, Staffordshire ST5 5BG 0782 621111

University of Kent at Canterbury, Kent CT2 7NZ 0227 764000

Lancaster University, University House, Bailrigg, Lancaster
LA1 4YW 0524 65201

University of Leeds, Woodhouse Lane, Leeds LS2 9JT
0532 333993

University of Leicester, University Road, Leicester LE1 7RH
0533 522522

University of Liverpool, PO Box 147, Liverpool L69 3BX
051-794 2000

London University: colleges, institutes and non-medical schools

Birkbeck College, Malet Street, London WC1E 7HX
071-580 6622

Courtauld Institute of Art, Somerset House, Strand, London
WC2R 0RN 071-873 0220

Goldsmiths' College, Lewisham Way, New Cross, London
SE14 6NW 081-692 7171

Heythrop College, 11–13 Cavendish Square, London
W1M 0AN 071-580 6941

Imperial College of Science, Technology and Medicine, South
Kensington, London SW7 2AZ 071-589 5111

Jews' College, Albert Road, Hendon, London NW4 2SJ
081-203 6427

King's College, Strand, London WC2R 2LS 071-836 5454

London School of Economics and Political Science, Houghton Street, London WC2A 2AE 071-405 7686

Queen Mary and Westfield College, Mile End Road, London E1 4NS 071-975 5555

Royal Holloway and Bedford New College, Egham Hill, Egham, Surrey TW20 0EX 0784 434455

Royal Veterinary College, Royal College Street, London NW1 0TU 071-387 2898

School of Oriental and African Studies, Thornhaugh Street, Russell Square, London WC1H 0XG 071-637 2388

School of Pharmacy, 29–39 Brunswick Square, London WC1N 1AX 071-753 5800

School of Slavonic and East European Studies, University of London WC1E 7HU 071-637 4934

University College, Gower Street, London WC1E 6BT 071-387 7050

Wye College, Ashford, Kent TN25 5AH 0233 812401

London University: medical and dental schools

Charing Cross and Westminster Medical School, St Dunstan's Road, London W6 8RP 081-846 7202

King's College School of Medicine and Dentistry, Bessemer Road, London SE5 9PJ 071-274 6222

London Hospital Medical College, Turner Street, London E1 2AD 071-377 7611

Royal Free Hospital School of Medicine, Rowland Hill Street, London NW3 2PF 071-794 0500 ext 4271

St Bartholomew's Hospital Medical College, West Smithfield, London EC1A 7BE 071-601 8834

St George's Hospital Medical School, Cranmer Terrace, Tooting, London SW17 0RE 081-672 9944

St Mary's Hospital Medical School, Norfolk Place, Paddington, London W2 1PG 071-723 1252

United Medical and Dental Schools of Guy's and St Thomas's Hospitals, Lambeth Palace Road, London SE1 7EH 071-922 8013

University College and Middlesex School of Medicine, University College, Gower Street, London WC1E 6BT 071-387 7050

London University: music schools
Royal Academy of Music, Marylebone Road, London NW1 5HT 071-935 5461

Royal College of Music, Prince Consort Road, London SW7 2BS 071-589 3643

University of London Senate House, Malet Street, London WC1E 7HU 071-636 8000

Loughborough University of Technology, Ashby Road, Leicestershire LE11 3TU 0509 263171

University of Manchester, Manchester M13 9PL 061-275 2074

University of Manchester Institute of Science and Technology
(UMIST), PO Box 88, Sackville Street, Manchester M60 1QD
061-236 3311

University of Newcastle upon Tyne, 6 Kensington Terrace,
Newcastle upon Tyne NE1 7RU 091-222 6000

University of Nottingham, University Park, Nottingham
NG7 2RD 0602 484848

Open University, PO Box 71, Walton Hall, Milton Keynes
MK7 6AG 0908 653231

University of Oxford, Admissions Office, Wellington Square,
Oxford OX1 2JD 0865 270207

University of Reading, Whiteknights House, Reading,
PO Box 217, RG6 2AH 0734 875123

University of Salford, The Cresent, Salford M5 4WT
061-745 5000

University of Sheffield, Sheffield S10 2TN
0742 768555 ext 4124

University of Southampton, Highfield, Southampton SO9 5NH
0703 595000

University of Surrey, Guildford, Surrey GU2 5XH 0483 300800

University of Sussex, Sussex House, Falmer, Brighton BN1 9RH
0273 678416

University of Warwick, Coventry, Warwickshire CV4 7AL
0203 523523

University of York, Heslington, York YO1 5DD 0904 433535

Northern Ireland
The Queen's University of Belfast, Belfast BT7 1NN
0232 245133

University of Ulster, Cromore Road, Coleraine, County Londonderry BT52 1SA 0265 44141

Scotland
University of Aberdeen, Regent Walk, Aberdeen AB9 1FX
0224 273504

University of Dundee, Dundee DD1 4HN 0382 23181

University of Edinburgh, Old College, South Bridge, Edinburgh EH8 9YL 031- 650 1000

University of Glasgow, University Avenue, Glasgow G12 8QQ
041-339 8855

Heriot-Watt University, Riccarton, Edinburgh EH14 4AS
031-449 5111

University of St Andrews, College Gate, St Andrews KY16 9AJ
0334 76161

University of Stirling, Stirling FK9 4LA 0786 73171

University of Strathclyde, Richmond Street, Glasgow G1 1XQ
041-553 4170/1/2/3

Wales

University College of Wales, Aberystwyth, PO Box 2, Aberystwyth, Dyfed SY23 2AX 0970 622021

University of Wales, Bangor, Gwynedd LL57 2DG 0248 351151

University of Wales College of Cardiff, PO Box 68, Cathays Park, Cardiff CF1 3AX 0222 874412

University of Wales College of Medicine, Heath Park, Cardiff CF4 4XN 0222 747747

St David's University College, Lampeter, Dyfed SA48 7ED 0570 422351

University College of Swansea, Singleton Park, Swansea SA2 8PP 0792 205678

II 'New' Universities

Anglia Polytechnic University, East Road, Cambridge CB1 1PF 0223 62271 and at Victoria Road South, Chelmsford CM15 1LL 0245 493131

Bournemouth University, Poole House, Talbot Campus, Fern Barrow, Poole, Dorset BH12 5BB 0202 524111

University of Brighton, Lewes Road, Brighton BN2 4GJ 0273 600900

University of Central England in Birmingham, Perry Barr, Birmingham B42 2SU 021-331 5000

London Guildhall University, Admissions office, 139 Minories, London EC3N 1NL 071-320 1000

Coventry University, Priory Street, Coventry CV1 5FB
0203 631313

De Montfort University, PO Box 143, Leicester LE1 9BH
0533 551551

Derbyshire University, Kedleston Road, Derby DE3 1GB
0332 47181

University of East London, Longbridge Road, Dagenham, Essex
RM8 2AS 081-590 7722

University of Glamorgan, Llantwit Road, Pontypridd, Mid
Glamorgan CF37 1DL 0443 480480

Glasgow Caledonian University, 70 Cowcaddens Road,
Glasgow G4 0BA 041-331 3330

University of Greenwich, Wellington Street, Woolwich, London
SE18 6PF 081-316 8590

University of Hertfordshire, PO Box 109, College Lane,
Hatfield, Hertfordshire AL10 9AB 0707 284000

University of Huddersfield, Queensgate, Huddersfield
HD1 3DH 0484 422288

University of Humberside, Beverley Road, Hull HU6 7HT
0482 440550

Kingston University, Penrhyn Road, Kingston upon Thames,
Surrey KT1 2EE 081-547 2000

University of Central Lancashire, Preston PR1 2TQ
0772 892000

Leeds Metropolitan University, Calverley Street, Leeds LS1 3HE
0532 832600

Liverpool John Moores University, 15–21 Webster Street,
Liverpool L3 2ET 051-207 3581

Manchester Metropolitan University, All Saints, Oxford Road,
Manchester M15 6BH 061-247 2000

Middlesex University, All Saints, White Hart Lane, London
N17 8HR 081-368 1299

Napier University, 219 Colinton Road, Edinburgh EH4 1DJ
031- 445 4330

University of North London, Holloway Road, London N7 8DB
071- 607 2789

University of Northumbria at Newcastle, Ellison Building, Ellison
Place, Newcastle upon Tyne NE1 8ST 091 232 6002 ext 4063/4

Nottingham Trent University, Burton Street, Nottingham
NG1 4BU 0602 418418

Oxford Brookes University, Gipsy Lane, Headington, Oxford
OX3 0BP 0865 741111

University of Paisley, High Street, Paisley PA1 2BE 041-848 3688

University of Plymouth, Drake Circus, Plymouth PL4 8AA
0752 600600

University of Portsmouth, Winston Churchill Avenue,
Portsmouth PO1 2EP 0705 827681

The Robert Gordon University, Schoolhill, Aberdeen AB9 1FR
0224 633611

University College Salford, Frederick Road, Salford M6 6PU
061-736 6541

Sheffield Hallam University, Pond Street, Sheffield S1 1WB
0742 720911

South Bank University, Borough Road, London SE1 0AA
071-928 8989

Staffordshire University, College Road, Stoke-on-Trent ST4 2DE
0782 744531

University of Sunderland, Langham Tower, Ryhope Road,
Sunderland SR2 7EE 091 515 2000

University of Teesside, Borough Road, Middlesbrough, Cleveland
TS1 3BA 0642 218121

Thames Valley University, St Mary's Road, Ealing, London
W5 5RF 081-579 5000 and at Wellington Street, Slough,
Berkshire SL1 1YG 0753 697513

University of the West of England, Bristol, Coldharbour Lane,
Frenchay, Bristol BS16 1QYT 0272 656261

University of Westminster, 309 Regent Street, London W1R 8AL
071-911 5000

University of Wolverhampton, Wulfruna Street, Wolverhampton
WV1 1SB 0902 321000

III Scottish Centrally Funded Colleges

Craigie College of Education, Beech Grove, Ayr KA8 OSR
The Admissions Officer Tel: 0292 260321

Duncan of Jordanstone College of Art, Perth Road, Dundee
DD1 4HT The Student Services Office Tel: 0382 23261

Dundee Institute of Technology, Bell Street, Dundee DD1 1HG
The Registry Tel: 0382 308000 ext 8043/4

Edinburgh College of Art, Lauriston Place, Edinburgh EH3 9DF
The College Registrar Tel: 031-229 9311 ext 235

Glasgow Caledonian University, 70 Cowcaddens Road,
Glasgow G4 OBA The Registrar Tel: 041-331 3330

Glasgow School of Art, 167 Renfrew Street, Glasgow G3 6RQ
Admissions Office Tel: 041-332 9797 ext 453

Jordanhill College of Education, 76 Southbrae Drive,
Glasgow G13 1PP The Registrar Tel: 041-950 3243/46

Moray House Institute of Education, (incorporating The
Scottish Centre for Physical Education, Movement and Leisure
Studies) Holyrood Road, Edinburgh EH8 8AQ
The Registry Tel: 031-556 8455

Napier University, 219 Colinton Road, Edinburgh EH14 1DJ
The Information Office, Freepost, Edinburgh EH14 OPA
Tel: 031-455 4330 Post-application enquiries only to
The Admissions Officer Tel: 031-455 4275

Northern College of Education, Hilton Place, Aberdeen
AB9 1FA The Registrar Tel: 0224 283500

University of Paisley, High Street, Paisley PA1 2BE The Students Records and Admissions Office Tel: 041-848 3688

Queen Margaret College, Clerwood Terrace, Edinburgh EH12 8TS The Admissions Office Tel: 031-317 3247

The Robert Gordon University, Schoolhill, Aberdeen AB9 1 FR
The Assistant Registrar (Student Administration)
Tel: 0224 633611 ext 201

Royal Scottish Academy of Music and Drama,
100 Renfrew Street, Glasgow G2 3DB The Secretary and Treasurer Tel: 041-332 4101

St Andrew's College of Education, (National Roman Catholic Teacher-Training College) Duntocher Road, Bearsden, Glasgow G61 4QA The Admissions Officer Tel: 041-943 1424

The Scottish Agricultural College, Cleeve Gardens, Oakbank Road, Perth PH1 1HF The Academic Registry Auchincruive Tel: 0292 520331 ext 280

Scottish College of Textiles, Netherdale. Galashiels TD1 3HF Assistant Secretary (Academic) Tel: 0896 3351 ext 2132

IV Colleges and Institutes of Higher Education

Bangor Normal College, Bangor, Gwynedd LL57 2PX
0248 370171

Bath College of Higher Education (incorporating Bath Academy of Art), Newton Park, Newton St Loe, Bath BA2 9BN
0225 873701

Bedford College of Higher Education, Cauldwell Street, Bedford MK42 9AH 0234 345151

Bishop Grosseteste College, Newport, Lincoln LN1 3DY 0522 527347

Bolton Institute of Higher Education, Deane Road, Bolton BL3 5AB 0204 28851

Bradford and Ilkley Community College, Great Horton Road, Bradford, West Yorkshire BD7 1AY 0274 753026

Bretton Hall College, Bretton Hall, West Bretton, Wakefield, West Yorkshire WF4 4LG 0924 830261

Buckinghamshire College of Higher Education, Queen Alexandra Road, High Wycombe, Buckinghamshire HP11 2JZ 0494 522141

Camborne School of Mines, Trevenson, Pool, Redruth, Cornwall TR15 3SE 0209 716977

Canterbury Christ Church College, North Holmes Road, Canterbury CT1 1QU 0227 767700

Cardiff Institute of Higher Education, PO Box 377, Western Avenue, Llandaff, Cardiff CF5 2SG 0222 551111

Central School of Speech and Drama, Embassy Theatre, 64 Eton Avenue, London NW3 3HY 071-722 8183

Charlotte Mason College, Rydal Road, Ambleside, Cumbria LA22 9BB 05394 33066

Cheltenham and Gloucester College of Higher Education,
The Park Campus, PO Box 220, The Park, Cheltenham
GL50 2QF 0242 532700

Chester College, Cheyney Road, Chester CH1 4BJ 0244 375444

Colchester Institute, Sheepen Road, Colchester, Essex C03 3LL
0206 761660

College of Physiotherapy, Aberfield Road, Pinderfields,
Wakefield WF1 4DG 0924 375217 ext 2275

College of St Mark and St John, Derriford Road, Plymouth
PL6 8BH 0752 777188

College of Ripon and York St John, Lord Mayor's Walk,
York Y03 7EX 0904 656771

Crewe and Alsager College of Higher Education, Crewe
Green Road, Crewe, Cheshire CW1 1DU 0270 500661

Dartington College of Arts, Higher Close, Dartington, Totnes,
Devon TQ9 6EJ 0803 862224

Doncaster College, Waterdale, Doncaster, South Yorkshire
DN1 3EX 0302 322122 ext 229

Edge Hill College of Higher Education, St Helen's Road,
Ormskirk L39 4QP 0695 575171

Falmouth School of Art and Design, Woodland, Falmouth,
Cornwall TR11 4RA 0326 211077

Farnborough College of Technology, Boundary Road,
Farnborough, Hampshire GU14 6SB 0252 515511

Gwent College of Higher Education, Allt-yr-yn-Avenue, Newport, Gwent NP9 5XA 0633 432432

Harper Adams Agricultural College, Edgmond, Newport, Shropshire TF10 8NB 0952 820280

Kent Institute of Art and Design, Oakwood Park, Oakwood Road, Maidstone, Kent ME16 8AG 0622 757286

King Alfred's College of Higher Education, Sparkford Road, Winchester S022 4NR 0962 841515

La Sainte Union College of Higher Education, The Avenue, Southampton S09 5HB 0703 228761

Liverpool Institute of Higher Education, PO Box 6, Stand Park Road, Liverpool L16 9JD 051-737 3000

The London Institute, 388-396 Oxford Street, London W1R IFE 071-491 8533

Luton College of Higher Education, Park Square, Luton, Bedfordshire LUI 3JU 0582 34111

Nene College, Moulton Park, Northampton NN2 7AL
0604 715000

New College, Framwellgate Moor Centre, Durham DH1 5ES
091 386 2421

Newman and Westhill Colleges, Genners Lane, Bartley Green, Birmingham B32 3NT 021-476 1181 and Westhill College, Selly Oak, Birmingham B29 6LL 021-472 7245

North Cheshire College, Padgate, Fearnhead, Warrington
WA2 0DB 0925 814343

North East Wales Institute of Higher Education, Plas Coch,
Mold Road, Wrexham, Clwyd LL13 2AW 0978 290666

North Riding College, Filey Road, Scarborough,
North Yorkshire YO11 3AZ 0723 362392

Norwich City College, Ipswich Road, Norwich NR2 2LJ
0603 660011

Ravensbourne College of Design and Communication, Walden
Road, Elmstead Woods, Chislehurst, Kent 081-468 7071

Roehampton Institute, Senate House, Roehampton Lane,
London SW15 5PU 081-878 8117

St Loye's School of Occupational Therapy, Topsham Road,
Exeter EX2 6ES 0392 219774

St Martin's College, Bowerham Road, Lancaster LA1 3JD
0524 63446

St Mary's College, Strawberry Hill, Waldegrave Road,
Twickenham, Middlesex TW1 4SX 081-892 0051

Southampton Institute of Higher Education, East Park Terrace,
Southampton SO9 4WW 0703 229381

South Devon College of Arts and Technology, Newton Road,
Torquay TQ2 5BY 0803 213242

Suffolk College, Rope Walk, Ipswich, Suffolk IP4 1LT
0473 255885

Swansea Institute of Higher Education, Townhill Road, Swansea, West Glamorgan SA2 0UT 0792 203482

Trinity and All Saints' College, Brownberrie Lane, Horsforth, Leeds LS18 5HD 0532 584341

Trinity College, College Road, Carmarthen, Dyfed SA3 3EP 0267 237971

University College, Frederick Road, Salford M6 6UP 061-736 6541

Welsh Agricultural College, Llanbadarn Fawr, Aberystwyth, Dyfed SY23 3AL 0970 624471

Welsh College of Music and Drama, Castle Ground, Cathays Park, Cardiff CF1 3ER 0222 342854

West Herts College, Hempstead Road, Watford WD1 3EZ 0923 257500

West London Institute of Higher Education, Gordon House, 300 St Margaret's Road, Twickenham TW1 1PT 081-891 0121

West Surrey College of Art and Design, Falkner Road, The Hart, Farnham, Surrey GU9 7DS 0252 722441

West Sussex Institute of Higher Education, The Dome, Upper Bognor Road, Bognor Regis PO21 1HR 0243 865581

Westminster College, North Hinksey, Oxford OX2 9AT 0865 247644

Winchester School of Art, Park Avenue, Winchester, Hampshire SO23 8DL 0962 842500

Worcester College of Higher Education, Henwick Grove, Worcester WR2 6AJ 0905 748080

Writtle College, Chelmsford, Essex CM1 3RR 0245 420705

Colleges affiliated with universities

Some colleges are affiliated to universities; many of them were formerly teacher-training and higher education colleges. Those linked to universities are:

	Affiliated university
Bishop Grossteste College Lincoln	Hull
Bradford and Ilkley College, Bradford	Bradford
Bretton Hall, Wakefield	Leeds
Charlotte Mason College, Cumbria Chester College	Lancaster Liverpool
Doncaster College	Leeds
Edge Hill College of HE, Ormskirk	Lancaster
King Alfred's College, Winchester	Southampton
La Sainte Union College of HE, Southampton	Southampton
Liverpool Institute of HE	Liverpool
Newman and Westhill Colleges, Birmingham	Birmingham

North Riding College, Scarborough	Leeds
College of Physiotherapy, Pinderfields, Wakefield	Leeds
Ripon and York St John College	Leeds
Roehampton Institute, London	Surrey
St Loye's School of Occupational Therapy, Exeter	Exeter
St Mark and St John College, Plymouth	Exeter
St Martin's College, Lancaster	Lancaster
St Mary's College, Twickenham	Surrey
Trinity and All Saints' College, Leeds	Leeds
Westminster College	Oxford
West Sussex Insitute of HE	Southampton
Winchester College of Art	Southampton

Glossary of Terms and Abbreviations

ACCESS COURSES Courses specially designed to help mature students who may not have any formal academic qualifications to enter higher education, provided by adult, further and higher education institutions.

ACCESS FUNDS Grants available to assist mature students on access or pre-entry courses. The grants are administered by FE/HE colleges.

ADAR The Art and Design Admissions Registry. Applications for degree courses and BTEC HND courses in art and design should be sent to the Registry between early February and the end of March.

ASSESSMENT, CONTINUOUS A method of assessment whereby course work, phased tests and exams are taken into account, either in a yearly assessment or as a contribution towards a final award.

BTEC Business and Technology Education Council. The body responsible for approving vocational courses at several levels – first, national and higher national, leading to nationally recognised awards.

CAREER DEVELOPMENT LOANS Loans administered by the banks with the Department of Employment. Available to assist students on vocational training courses.

CATS Credit Accumulation and Transfer. Course applicants can be given 'credit' for experience, training and qualifications gained previously. This 'credit' is put on a record of achievement or 'accumulation'; and there is a 'transfer' when the applicant formally applies for a course, and, if successful, moves from his or her job. Contact ECCTIS (qv) for a copy of *The Students' Guide to Educational Credit Transfer.*

CENTRALLY FUNDED COLLEGES Higher education colleges in Scotland, similar to polytechnics. Some of the colleges became university institutions under the 1992 Further and Higher Education Act. They provide a variety of courses leading to degrees, higher diplomas, diplomas and certificates.

CITY AND GUILDS OF LONDON INSTITUTE (City and Guilds) A national organisation which awards certificates and diplomas in vocational subjects provided at FE colleges.

CLEARING Procedures are run by UCAS from mid-August until late September each year. The schemes assist students whose original applications were unsuccessful to find vacancies. Also for applicants who did not apply at the normal time, or whose A-level and/or AS grades were below the requirement set by their first-choice institution.

CONDITIONAL OFFER An offer from an institution of a place, conditional upon the applicant attaining certain examination grades. It is worth while, however, contacting the institution in cases of failure to reach the required standard; demand for and supply of places does vary from year to year.

COUNCIL TAX The tax is based on the value of property owned or lived in. Student premises will be exempt. Students living with their parents or with other non-students are eligible for the personal discount of 25 per cent.

DIPLOMA OF HIGHER EDUCATION (DipHE) A two-year programme of work across several subjects chosen from a wide selection of options to provide a degree-level course for students who do not yet want to specialise. The entry level is the same as for a degree course – two A-levels.

DISCRETIONARY AWARDS These awards, which are now rare, are made 'at the discretion' of the organisation, usually an LEA, to assist students who do not benefit from other awards.

ECCTIS 2000 Information service on computer which is provided by the Department for Education. It carries information on its database of courses, professional bodies, qualifications and employers. Information on HE courses can be accessed by subject; type of courses; method of study; institution type; institution location; institution name; UCAS course code; ECCTIS reference number.

ERASMUS This scheme – the European Community Action Scheme for the Mobility of University Students – provides grants for students studying for part of their degree or diploma course in another European Community institution or country. Credits are given for completed periods of study.

MANDATORY AWARD All students of 18 or over who have been offered a place on an advanced or higher education course qualify for consideration for a mandatory award. Amounts are based on various criteria including parents' earnings, and LEAs should be contacted for up-to-date information.

MATURE STUDENTS Students aged 21 and over at the start of their course who thus qualify for special financial consideration.

PGCE Postgraduate Certificate of Education. A one-year full-time course for graduates, enabling them to qualify as trained teachers.

PROFESSIONAL COURSES These courses are offered at colleges and some universities. They lead to, or give exemption from, the examinations of professional institutions in such areas as law, insurance, personnel management and engineering.

SANDWICH COURSES These can be either 'thin' or 'thick'. Thin courses include more than one period of industrial experience. A thick sandwich course usually consists of two years in college, then one full year in industry, followed by a fourth year in college.

SCOTVEC The Scottish Vocational Education Council which approves vocational courses in Scotland run by colleges, schools and universities.

SPONSORSHIP Various schemes by which companies, organisations and the Services support students with bursaries, industrial training placements or research facilities.

UCAS The Universities and Colleges Admissions Service which controls the system of first degree and HND applications to universities and colleges.

VOCATIONAL COURSES These courses lead to a qualification with direct relevance to a job or career – for example, construction, engineering, business studies, advertising, accounting and journalism. Entry levels vary from two A-levels or equivalent to two GCSE subjects depending on the course applied for.

Hobsons' Student Helpbook Series

THIS SERIES OF ADVICE PUBLICATIONS is designed to help students of all ages make the right choices about their careers and education.

The books raise the issues which must be considered, give straightforward guidance and point to sources of information on further and higher education, careers and training.

Their lively style, with most of the titles including cartoons, make them ideal for students to read for themselves. Many careers teachers, post-16 advisers and parents will also find them a valuable source of reference.

Jobs and Careers After A-Levels
Anne Purdon
(Listed as part of the Government's Careers Library Initiative)

Jobs and Careers After A-Levels covers information about jobs open to people with A-level passes – where to find them and how to get them. It also homes in on training – availability, duration, and applicability to a future career.

Career profiles trace the experiences of recent A-level students and a whole chapter is devoted to where to look for further helpful information.

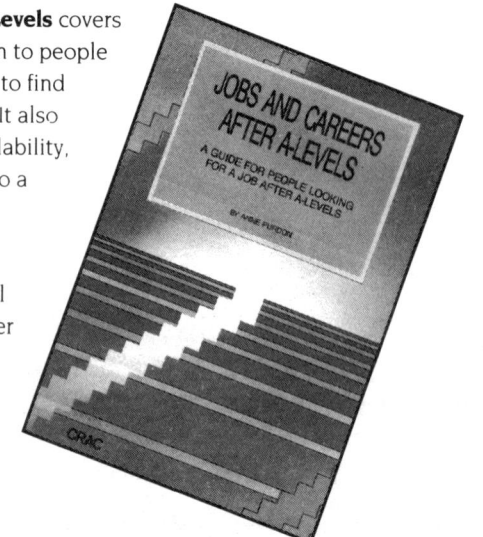

PRICE: £6.99

NEW! Studying in Europe
Written by Anne Bariet and Olivier Rollot
Adapted by William Archer

Taking a higher education course in Europe often widens the scope for a challenging and lucrative career. This book opens the doors of the universities of Europe and sets out the issues to resolve before embarking on studying across the Channel.
Studying in Europe gives all the information students need to choose the establishments that offer the right course and the town or city. This book includes all the European exchange programmes such as COMETT and ERASMUS which can ease the transition. And finally, it contains hundreds of addresses: all the contacts needed to locate the European university best suited to the student's needs.

PRICE: £6.99   Publication: Summer 1993

Hard Cash!
Alan Jamieson

A guide to financial survival for all students supporting themselves, covering working opportunities and sources of funding.

Hard Cash! explains all sources of funds: grants, sponsorship, charities, Student Loans, Access Funds, Career Development Loans, the banks and relatives. A chapter is devoted to each. Self-help is the solution proposed in Part 2, where 21 students share their entrepreneurial ideas and experiences. Their suggestions include waitressing in the Alps, teaching in Singapore, bar work, washing-up, windsurfing lessons, a dress hire agency and more.

PRICE: £6.99

NEW EDITION COMING AUTUMN 1993 Decisions at 17/18+

Michael Smith and Veronica Matthew
(Listed as part of the Government's Careers Library Initiative)

Designed with the school and college-leaver in mind, **Decisions at 17/18+** helps the student look forward into the next decade as well as examining what is available in the immediate future. It weighs up the options on offer after the sixth-form and shows where chosen subjects might lead.

Each course of action can have its own special attractions and discovering the best route means considering personality, academic record, financial resources and employment opportunities.

PRICE £6.99   Publication: Autumn 1993

A Year Off...A Year On?

A Year Off...A Year On? is designed to help students get the best from a year off. It is packed with information, ideas and useful addresses to help make the time productive for young people, and an asset for future study or careers. The information has been thoroughly updated for this new edition.

Includes: ◆ Adventure holidays
◆ Working holidays
◆ Conservation projects
◆ Voluntary and paid work in Britain and abroad ◆ Personal accounts of 'year-outers'

PRICE: £6.99

Decisions at 15/16+
Michael Smith and Veronica Matthew
(Listed as part of the Government's
Careers Library Initiative)

Decisions at 15/16+ is for students looking ahead to GCSEs and life after school. It begins with the challenges of homework, revision and exams. It stresses the value of gaining skills and the right attitudes alongside qualifications – employers are looking for all three.

Every option at 16 is explained and weighed up to help students decide which path to take.

◆ Vocational training in industry or college ◆ Full-time study, opening the way to higher education ◆ Youth training
◆ A permanent job ◆ NVQs ◆ People at work and the types of job they do ◆ Technological changes

PRICE: £6.99

NEW EDITION! Decisions at 13/14+
Michael Smith and Veronica Matthew
(Listed as part of the Government's Careers Library Initiative)

To make the right choice of GCSE courses students need information. For many it is their first experience of making decisions which will affect their future. **Decisions at 13/14+** begins with a guide to decision-making. It goes on to give facts on every subject students are likely to encounter. It encourages forward thinking by pointing the way to academic options after school and includes an A–Z look at areas of work.

◆ Every curriculum subject examined ◆ Commonly posed questions answered. 'Can I take GCSEs after the age of 16?' 'How many subjects do I have to study?' ◆ An insight into what's involved in the exams ◆ Records of achievement ◆ Resits ◆ TVEI, NVQs and vocational education ◆ What's next? BTEC, A-levels ◆ Which subjects are prerequisites for specific careers? ◆ How to avoid closing career doors ◆ An A–Z guide to careers: descriptions, qualifications, further information and reading

PRICE: £6.99

Career Opportunities for Anyone
Anne Purdon
(Listed as part of the Government's Careers Library Initiative)

It's no secret that the right job is difficult to find and if you don't have a string of high GCSE passes it is even harder. **Career Opportunities for Anyone** has been written for school-leavers without academic qualifications and gives practical ideas and help on how to find a job. Topics covered include:

◆ Assessing your own skills and abilities ◆ Different types of jobs available ◆ Apprenticeships ◆ Youth training ◆ Working for yourself ◆ Working abroad

PRICE: £4.99

NEW EDITION!
Your Choice of A-Levels
Mary Munro and Alan Jamieson
(Listed as part of the Government's Careers Library Initiative)
Essential reading for all Year 11 students considering A-level and AS.

Experts closely involved with A-level and AS work have written and updated each of the subject chapters, explaining what is required of the students and what the students can expect from the various subjects.

Includes the latest information on course content and combinations of subjects; teaching and learning methods; examinations and assessment; entry into higher education and careers, and a full listing of AS subjects.

PRICE: £8.99 Publication: October 1993

**ALSO AVAILABLE:
The Career Counsellors' Job Book and Further and Higher Education Guide 1994**
(Listed as part of the Government's Careers Library Initiative)

An invaluable source book of information for school-leavers on employers and job opportunities. The A–Z directory of employers lists details of over 1,200 companies with many of them giving further information in their employer profiles. Special sections also cover areas such as training routes, sponsorship, higher education, nursing and paramedical careers.

◆ Practical advice on how to apply for jobs
◆ Includes a unique guide to careers in healthcare
◆ The only school-leaver's employment and training directory available

PRICE: £20.00 Publication: September 1993